Gold Run Snowmobile, Inc.
Computerized Business Simulation
Windows® Version, CD-ROM

Third Edition

Sales, Service, and Storage of Snowmobiles

Leland Mansuetti
Sierra College

Keith Weidkamp
Sierra College

Boston   Burr Ridge, IL   Dubuque, IA   Madison, WI   New York   San Francisco   St. Louis
Bangkok   Bogotá   Caracas   Lisbon   London   Madrid
Mexico City   Milan   New Delhi   Seoul   Singapore   Sydney   Taipei   Toronto

Irwin/McGraw-Hill

A Division of The McGraw·Hill Companies

GOLD RUN SNOWMOBILE, INC.: COMPUTERIZED BUSINESS SIMULATION

Copyright © 1999 by The McGraw-Hill Companies, Inc. All rights reserved.
Printed in the United States of America.
The contents of, or parts thereof, may be reproduced for use with
GOLD RUN SNOWMOBILE, INC
Computerized Business Simulation
Leland Mansuetti and Keith Weidkamp
provided such reproductions bear copyright notice and may not be reproduced in
any form for any other purpose without permission of the publisher.

2 3 4 5 6 7 8 9 0 BKM/BKM 9 0 9 8 7 6 5 4 3 2 1 0

Manual ISBN 0-07-234306-0

http://www.mhhe.com

DEDICATED TO OUR FAMILIES

Janet

Linda, Aaron, Kristin, Zachary

ACKNOWLEDGMENTS

A Special Thanks To
Joanna Margala and Stacey Lucksinger
for all of their help and support
in the development of this project.

The Accounting Students of Sierra College
Rocklin, California

PREFACE

The **Gold Run Snowmobile, Incorporated,** computerized business simulation has been designed with two important objectives in mind. First, the student will receive a thorough review of all the major accounting concepts found in the introductory chapters of <u>Financial Accounting</u> and <u>Principles of Accounting</u>. While reviewing these concepts the student will become familiar with a computerized accounting system similar to commercial systems.

Sophisticated, yet easy to use, software will allow the student to work very quickly and efficiently through a variety of business transactions. At the end of each session (7 days and 18-26 transactions) the student will find a convenient **"Check It Out"** block to compare account balances and trial balance totals. If errors are found, the student will simply follow the audit trail provided, locate the errors, and make the necessary corrections. The **Mid-Project Evaluation** (December 17) and **Final Evaluation** (at the end of the fourth quarter, December 31), will be performed by printing selected documents and answering a series of analytical questions. This process will provide a detailed review of the financial information. *Time originally spent preparing the documents manually will now be spent evaluating the statements and the business operations.*

The **Gold Run Snowmobile, Inc.**, accounting system is designed in a Windows format. Data entry is accomplished using a general journal screen for journalizing and validation. After entering the date, the chart of accounts is accessed with a mouse click. The chart may be used directly for data entry or each account may be entered manually. A calculator is available for immediate calculation of amounts to be entered and the calculated total may be "pasted" directly into a debit or credit entry. The amount of the credit entry can be automatically entered using the **C Key**. Printing documents for review and analysis is quick and easy. The general journal (all or part), general ledger, accounts receivable and accounts payable ledgers, and all inventory records can be brought to the screen for quick review and/or printing. These printed documents, as well as the multiple-step financial statements, provide the information for a detailed analysis of the business operations.

Special features of the business simulation include an **automatic closing** option which allows the student to close the books quickly and efficiently with a single keystroke. The closing entry procedure, which is so time consuming when completed manually, is similar to many commercial systems. A **reinstatement option** allows the student to reopen the accounts, if necessary, for error correction purposes. This allows better use of time for important analysis and evaluation of the Gold Run Snowmobile, Incorporated, operations. A new **Reset** option allows the student to reset the disk back to the December 3 beginning balances any time prior to the start of the second week of transactions.

The overall objective of this practice set is to provide students an opportunity to use, review, and learn a very significant amount of financial/corporate accounting information in a very short period of time. Using this computerized accounting system allows the students to fully realize this objective, maximize their study time, and to move closer to the real world accounting and finance environment.

Leland Mansuetti

Keith Weidkamp

TABLE OF CONTENTS

Introduction to Gold Run Snowmobile, Inc. 1

Chart of Accounts 2

    Account List 7

    Customer and Vendor Lists 10

KEY DETAILS TO REMEMBER AS YOU JOURNALIZE TRANSACTIONS ... 11

Installing The Program and Beginning The Transactions 13

    Installation Using the CD-ROM Disk 14

    Installation Using the Program Disks (3) 14

    Creating the Data Disk 14

    Begin the Program and Enter the Data 15

    Transactions for the Week of December 4-10, 2001 16

    "Check It Out" Block 27

ERROR CORRECTION PROCEDURES 28

Transactions for December 11-17, 2001 29

    "Check It Out" Block 36

    Print List 37

MID-PROJECT EVALUATION 39

Transactions for December 18-24, 2001 47

    "Check It Out" Block 55

Transactions for December 26-31, 2001 57

    "Check It Out" Block 65

Bank Reconciliation 66

ADJUSTING AND CLOSING ENTRIES 69

    Adjusting Entries for the Quarter Ended,
    December 31, 2001 70

    Print List 72

    Closing Entries for the Quarter Ended,
    December 31, 2001 73

    Error Correction After Closing the Books 73

FINAL EVALUATION 75

Appendix 83

An Introduction To
GOLD RUN SNOWMOBILE, INC.

Gold Run Snowmobile, Incorporated is a small corporation, locally owned by several stockholders who are interested in safe snowmobiling as a sport and in the snowmobiling business as a strong business investment. Dennis O'Hannah and Brenda Jenner, major stockholders in the company, are also salaried executives with full responsibility for its operations. The business, located near Thunder Mountain and Lake Tahoe, is an exclusive dealer for Trail-Tracker Snowmobiles. The business also sells several other brands of snowmobiles and provides excellent service for all snowmobiles, including parts and labor. The business rents storage space to those customers who prefer to keep their snowmobile equipment in the mountains and close to the trails. Dennis and Brenda, avid winter sports enthusiasts, are directly involved in trail and vehicle safety instruction. They also participate regularly in snowmobile races as sponsors and, occasionally, as veteran racers.

To complete the on-the-job training requirement for your accounting course, you have been placed in a four-week internship program with Gold Run Snowmobile, Inc. You will be responsible for all of the accounting work from December 4 through December 31, including recording the transactions, auditing your work, and correcting all errors. Your internship will also require the printing and preparation of the financial statements, analysis of the statements and business operations, and the closing of the books at the end of the fourth quarter, December 31, 2001. Since Gold Run Snowmobile uses a computerized accounting system, this opportunity to obtain hands on experience and practice your accounting skills should be very rewarding and exciting.

The first step in operating the computerized system correctly is to review the chart of accounts. **A clear understanding** of how certain accounts are used by Gold Run Snowmobile, Inc., **is required before you begin the recording process**. A detailed explanation of how several accounts are used in this accounting system follows on the next five pages. Pages 7, 8, and 9 list the full **Chart of Accounts** and page 10 displays the **Customer List** and **Vendor List** with the account numbers used to identify these customers and businesses when entering the transactions. On pages 11 and 12 is a summary of the special keys that may be used in the data entry process and a review of important business facts that must be remembered when entering the transaction data.

CHART OF ACCOUNTS

To properly enter the accounting transactions for Gold Run Snowmobile, Inc., you will need to familiarize yourself with the chart of accounts for the business. The business has four revenue accounts: **Snowmobile, Accessories, and Parts Sales; Sales Returns & Allowances; Service Fees Earned; and Storage Fees Earned.**

Snowmobile, Accessories, and Parts Sales and **Sales Returns and Allowances** record all transactions involving the sale and return of merchandise items. **Service Fees Earned** accounts for fees earned in servicing customer snowmobiles and accessories. *Sales tax (7%) is charged on all merchandise and service sales.* The revenue account **Storage Fees Earned** is adjusted at the end of each accounting period to reflect all of the storage fees **that have been earned.** The liability account, **Unearned Storage Fees** is used to record all of the initial cash receipts for storage of customer snowmobiles, trailers, and equipment. *Sales tax is not charged on storage fees.*

Gold Run Snowmobile, Inc., uses a **perpetual inventory system.** All purchases and sales of merchandise transactions will include additional data entry regarding the quantity and the specific item(s) being purchased or sold. This information will be an automatic part of each journal entry where merchandise is involved. This will maintain a constant updated record of the quantity of all merchandise on hand and the total value of the inventory.

Gold Run Snowmobile, Inc., uses the **NET METHOD** to record all purchases of merchandise. All purchases from vendors who extend cash discounts are **recorded at the NET cost** (the list price less the discount). Example: An inventory item with a $1,200 list price and extended terms of 2/10, n/30 will be recorded as a debit to Merchandise Inventory for $1,176 ($1,200 x .98). All merchandise will be purchased on account and be credited to Accounts Payable. As each purchase invoice is paid on time, Accounts Payable will be debited and Cash credited. *On the rare occasion when a purchase invoice that offers a cash discount is, through error, not paid within the discount period, the discount will be lost.* This will require a debit to the **Discounts Lost account** and a credit to the **Accounts Payable account.** This credit to Accounts Payable will return the balance owed to the vendor to the full balance due (at list prices). This new, corrected balance will then be paid in cash.

Under the perpetual inventory system, when any snowmobiles or accessories are sold for cash, on credit, or through customer use of a bank or company credit card, **a second entry is required to update the general ledger accounts**. This second entry will include a **debit to Cost of Goods Sold** and a **credit to Merchandise Inventory** and WILL BE AUTOMATICALLY JOURNALIZED AND POSTED BY THE PROGRAM.

Gold Run Snowmobile accepts both **bank** credit cards and **company** credit cards. When a customer purchases merchandise using a bank credit card, the sale is entered as a **cash sale**. The credit card expense (1-4%) **is not** recorded at the time of the sale. For bank card charges the business is charged a credit card fee which is recorded when noted on the bank statement received at the end of the month. If a customer uses a company credit card, the sale is recorded as a sale on account with **Accounts Receivable, Credit Card Companies** being debited for the charge. This process maintains a record of all of the credit card company charges that are owed to Gold Run Snowmobile, Inc., until payment arrives from the credit card company. The credit card expense is recorded **when the cash payment is received from the credit card company.**

Several accounts which require special attention are listed below:

106 **Allowance for Doubtful Accounts** is the contra current asset account that is debited when accounts receivable are written off as bad debts.

107 **Accounts Receivable, Credit Card Companies** records all **company credit card** sales. When the cash is received from the credit card company, the credit card expense is recorded. (All bank card sales are recorded as **cash sales** with the credit card expense recorded at the end of the month after being charged by the bank.)

111 **Storage Fees Receivable** is used to record accrued storage fees.

115 **Merchandise Inventory** is the inventory account for all personal snowmobile, accessories, and parts. The perpetual inventory system will maintain a running balance of the Merchandise Inventory account as well as the exact quantity of each product stocked by Gold Run Snowmobile. The correct running balance of this account will be a major check figure given at the end of each week of data entry.

121 **Prepaid Insurance** is debited for the purchase of all insurance policies.

125 **Prepaid Advertising** is used only for adjusting entries. All advertising costs are debited directly to the Advertising Expense account.

127 **Store and Shop Supplies** is debited for all purchases of supplies. Check printing charges are also charged to this account.

145 **Leasehold Improvements** to the rented storage and service facilities have been made in the past and more are planned for the future. These permanent improvements technically become the property of the property owner upon installation to the rented facility. The cost of these improvements is amortized to the Rent Expense account over the life of the lease agreement.

150 **Land** owned by Gold Run Snowmobile is currently used only as a minor storage facility, but future plans call for construction of a new store and a major storage warehouse.

160 **Leasehold** is the account debited when a long-term sub-lease is signed. A portion of this leasehold is amortized to Rent Expense at the end of each quarter.

205 **Sales Tax Payable** records the **7% sales tax** that is charged for all merchandise sales, accessory and parts sales, *and service sales*. Sales tax is **not** charged on storage fees.

221 **Unearned Storage Fees** is credited directly for all storage fees received in advance. To keep a storage space, customers are required to pay their fees for at least three months in advance. Sales tax is **not** charged on storage fees.

311 **Dividends Declared** is debited for all official dividend declarations. At the end of each accounting period the account is closed to the Retained Earnings account.

411 **Service Fees Earned** is credited for all customer service and is billed at a rate of **$58.00** per hour.

421 **Storage Fees Earned** is adjusted at the end of the accounting period for all storage fees that **have been earned during the quarter**.

501 **Cost of Goods Sold** is the *Cost Account* that is debited for the cost of each item sold. Under the perpetual inventory system, with each sale of merchandise, Cost of Goods Sold is debited and Merchandise is credited. With each sales return of merchandise, Merchandise is debited and Cost of Goods Sold is credited. As each sale or sales return entry is entered and the merchandise inventory involved is identified, the program will automatically record the entry to update the Cost of Goods Sold and the Merchandise Inventory accounts.

505 **Transportation-In** is the *Cost Account* debited for all freight and delivery charges incurred in transporting merchandise to the Gold Run Snowmobile, Inc., receiving dock. Most of the shipments of merchandise to Gold Run are with FOB destination terms. The few shipments received with FOB shipping point (FOB factory) terms are charged to the Transportation-In account. The amounts charged to Transportation-In (usually not material) are added to the Cost of Goods Sold when calculating the Gross Profit of the business. Deliveries of merchandise items to customers are charged to **Delivery Expense**. Freight charges for the delivery of assets to the business are charged directly as an additional cost of the asset account.

602 **Store and Shop Supplies Expense** is used only for adjusting entries.

604 **Advertising Expense** is debited directly for all advertising fees incurred.

606 **Delivery Expense** is an **Operating Expense Account** debited for the delivery and freight charges incurred in shipping <u>merchandise items</u> to customers.

607 **Credit Card Expense** accounts for the bank and company credit card fees charged to Gold Run Snowmobile, Inc., for allowing customers to use their credit cards to purchase merchandise and services. These fees will be between 1 and 4 percent of the total amount (including sales tax) of the customer charge. Credit card charges for the use of bank cards will be accounted for at the end of the month when received on the bank statement. Credit card charges for the use of company credit cards will be recorded when the cash is received from the credit card company. *An end-of-the-period adjustment will be made at the end of each quarter to account for accrued credit card charges on credit card company receivables that will be collected during the subsequent quarter.*

608	**Tools Expense** is debited for all small purchases of store and shop tools.
621	**Rent Expense** may be adjusted at the end of the accounting period for an amortized portion of the Leasehold Improvements account. Under a lease agreement, the regular monthly rent is paid by the business at the beginning of each month.
622	**Insurance Expense** is adjusted at the end of each accounting period.
623	**Bad Debt Expense** is estimated at the end of each quarter using the aging of accounts receivable method.
627	**Bank Service Charges** is debited for all service costs on the business checking account.
628	**License Expense** is debited for all business and vehicle license fees.
633	**Discounts Lost** is charged for the loss incurred when a purchase invoice, through error, is not paid on time (before the end of the discount period). When the NET purchases method is used to record the purchases of merchandise, an internal control system is established to insure that all invoices are paid in time to qualify for the discount. The Discounts Lost account should never have an entry if the control system is in place and is used properly. The Discounts Lost account is also referred to as the Purchases Discounts Lost account.
713	**Dividends Earned** is an **Other Revenue Account** that is credited for dividends earned on short-term investments.
721	**Gain on Sale of Assets** is an **Other Revenue Account** that is credited when the proceeds from the sale of a Plant and Equipment asset are greater than the book value of the asset. This account is **not used** in like-kind exchange (trade) transactions.
821	**Loss on Sale/Disposal of Assets** is an **Other Expense Account** that is debited when a Plant and Equipment asset is sold and the proceeds of the sale are less than the book value of the asset. This account is also used to account for the loss incurred when an asset **with book value** is donated or given away. For like-kind exchange (trade) transactions, this account is **not used** under normal circumstances. Only under unusual circumstances (a "material loss") might this account be used for a like-kind exchange.

When entering the transactions in the Gold Run Snowmobile accounting system, all of the accounts will be identified by account number. You will see the account title appear on the screen as you enter the account number. With the cursor at the account prompt, the **Chart of Accounts** may be displayed on the screen by clicking on the **Chart of Accounts** button. You may move through the chart using the scroll bar.

Special data entry procedures that will make your work very efficient have been built into the new Gold Run Snowmobile accounting system. These procedures will be introduced and explained in detail in the first few entries that you journalize for December 4, 5, and 6.

Detailed information on customer and vendor account activity and account balances will be maintained automatically in the Accounts Receivable and the Accounts Payable ledgers. Information will be recorded in the system by identifying each customer or vendor/creditor by number.

CHART OF ACCOUNTS
GOLD RUN SNOWMOBILE, INCORPORATED

ASSETS

101	Cash
102	Petty Cash
103	Short-Term Investments
105	Accounts Receivable
106	Allowance for Doubtful Accounts
107	Accounts Receivable, Credit Card Companies
109	Notes Receivable
111	Storage Fees Receivable
113	Interest Receivable
115	Merchandise Inventory
121	Prepaid Insurance
124	Prepaid Property Tax
125	Prepaid Advertising
127	Store and Shop Supplies
131	Store Equipment and Fixtures
132	Accumulated Depreciation, Store Equipment and Fixtures
135	Shop Equipment
136	Accumulated Depreciation, Shop Equipment
139	Trucks
140	Accumulated Depreciation, Trucks
145	Leasehold Improvements
150	Land
160	Leasehold

LIABILITIES

201	Accounts Payable
203	Notes Payable
204	Discount on Notes Payable
205	Sales Tax Payable
207	Dividends Payable
209	Salaries & Wages Payable
211	Estimated Property Taxes Payable
213	Income Taxes Payable
215	Interest Payable
221	Unearned Storage Fees
231	Long-term Lease Liability
232	Discount on Lease Financing

CHART OF ACCOUNTS
GOLD RUN SNOWMOBILE, INCORPORATED

STOCKHOLDERS' EQUITY

301   Common Stock
305   Retained Earnings
311   Dividends Declared

REVENUE

401   Snowmobile, Accessories, & Parts Sales
402   Sales Returns & Allowances
411   Service Fees Earned
421   Storage Fees Earned

COST OF GOODS SOLD

501   Cost of Goods Sold
505   Transportation-In

OPERATING EXPENSES

<u>Store And Shop Expenses</u>

601   Salaries & Wages Expense
602   Store & Shop Supplies Expense
603   Truck & Equipment Operating Expense
604   Advertising Expense
606   Delivery Expense
607   Credit Card Expense
608   Tools Expense
610   Depreciation Expense, Store Equipment & Fixtures
611   Depreciation Expense, Shop Equipment
612   Depreciation Expense, Trucks

CHART OF ACCOUNTS
GOLD RUN SNOWMOBILE, INCORPORATED

Administrative Expenses

621	Rent Expense
622	Insurance Expense
623	Bad Debt Expense
624	Property Tax Expense
625	Electric and Gas Expense
626	Telephone Expense
627	Bank Service Charges
628	License Expense
629	Professional Services Expense
631	Cash Short & Over
633	Discounts Lost
635	Miscellaneous Expense

OTHER REVENUE

711	Interest Earned
713	Dividends Earned
721	Gain on Sale of Assets
731	Gain on Short-Term Investments
741	Miscellaneous Revenue

OTHER EXPENSES

811	Income Tax Expense
813	Interest Expense
821	Loss on Sale/Disposal of Assets
831	Loss on Short-Term Investments

INCOME SUMMARY

901	Income Summary

Gold Run Snowmobile, Incorporated
Customer List

Customer Number	Customer
10400	Mary Bermuda
10450	Colfax Sno Katts
10750	Alice Cordero
10930	Downieville Dusters
11000	Chris Enburger
11250	Cathi Grobowski
11340	Beverly Kline
11470	Ray Norburg
11510	Karen Osetto
11675	Cheryl Papini
11780	Running Ramblers
11800	Snowbirds
11925	Thunder Mountain, Inc.
11950	Ruth Yates

Gold Run Snowmobile, Incorporated
Vendor List

Vendor Number	Vendor
20300	Buster Supply
21680	Butler & Kadnaso
22500	Fastwinn, Incorporated
23400	Inglass, Incorporated
24850	Morelli Sports Equipment
26500	Norton America
27000	Swift, Incorporated
28400	Trail-Tracker, Inc.
29650	Wind Dancer

KEY DETAILS TO REMEMBER AS YOU JOURNALIZE TRANSACTIONS

To properly and efficiently operate the computerized accounting system used by Gold Run Snowmobile, Inc., you must be familiar with several important computer procedures as well as business and account information details. These procedures and details are summarized in the list below:

Sales tax of **7%** is charged on all sales and labor. Sales tax is **not charged** on storage fees. When calculating sales tax, <u>round all amounts to the nearest cent</u> ($4.025768 = $4.03).

Credit Card Fees of **1% to 4%** will be assessed by banks and credit card companies. Bank credit card fees will be accounted for at the end of the month from information received on the bank statement. Credit card company fees will be recorded when the cash is received from the credit card company.

Labor charges will be billed to customers at a rate of **$58.00 per hour**. Where necessary, **round all calculations to the nearest cent**.

For all **interest calculations** use exact days and a 360-day banker's year. For all interest and discount calculations **round the interest or discount amount to the nearest cent**.

All sales or sales returns of merchandise items will require two entries. After the regular sales or sales return entry has been recorded and posted, the program will **automatically** record the second entry required with an update to the **Cost of Goods Sold** and the **Merchandise Inventory** accounts.

Inventory information is entered into the system for any journal entry that changes the quantity/value of the Merchandise Inventory account. When a journal entry for any sales, sales return, merchandise purchase, or merchandise return transaction is verified, the inventory information is then requested. When the inventory information matches the journal entry, **click on Post** and the general ledger, subsidiary ledger, and the inventory ledger will be updated.

The **NET method** is used to record all merchandise purchases. It is intended that all invoices be paid on time. If an error is made and an invoice is not paid on time, the cost of this error will be recorded in the **Discounts Lost** account.

All personal snowmobiles and snowmobile trailers carry a 25% markup on **net cost** (20% markup on selling price). All accessories carry a 100% markup on **net cost** (50% markup on selling price). **Example:** A snowmobile with a net cost of $5,000 would sell at retail for $6,250 ($5,000 x 1.25). An accessory with a net cost of $4.50 would sell at retail for $9.00.

Gold Run Snowmobile extends **30-day credit to all charge customers. Balances that are over the 30-day credit period are considered** <u>past due</u>.

When entering transactions, always use proper accounting procedure and enter the debit entries **first**. When **debits** equal **credits** you will have a complete transaction to verify.

If an error correction entry for cash requires a credit to cash and a check has not been issued, enter **ERROR** or **00000** as the check number.

An ERROR CORRECTION ENTRY with a credit to the Merchandise Inventory account will request a debit memo number. At the debit memo prompt enter **ERROR**.

You may terminate a journalizing session **at any time.** When you return to the journal entry process at a later time, the last entry recorded and posted will be displayed on the screen.

A December 3, 2001 Trial Balance, Schedule of Accounts Receivable, Schedule of Accounts Payable, and an Inventory Analysis are shown in the Appendix.

GOLD RUN SNOWMOBILE, INCORPORATED

INSTALLING THE PROGRAM

AND BEGINNING

THE TRANSACTIONS

INSTALLING THE PROGRAM

Installation Using the CD-ROM Disk:

1. **Close all applications that may be running (such as MS WinWord or MS Excell).**
2. Insert the **CD-ROM disk** in the appropriate drive.
3. Click on **Start,** then click on **Run**.
4. Type the letter of the disk drive, followed by **:\Setup**   Example: **D:\Setup**
5. Press the **Enter key**.
6. At the first prompt, click on **OK** if all applications have been closed.
7. At the next prompt, **click** on the button with the **monitor icon** to install the program on the default drive and folder, **C:\Program Files\goldrun**.
8. Click on **OK** when the installation has been completed.

Installation Using the Program Disks (3):

1. Insert **Disk #1** in **Drive A** (or **Drive B**).
2. Click on **Start** in the Task Bar.
3. Click on **Run**.
4. At the text box, type **A:\SETUP** (or **B:\SETUP**)
5. Click on **OK**.
6. When prompted, insert **Disk #2** in **Drive A** (or **Drive B**). Click on **OK**.
7. When prompted, Click on the **large icon** in the upper left corner of the dialogue box.
8. When prompted, insert **Disk #3** in **Drive A** (or **Drive B**), then Click on **OK**.
9. Click on **OK** when the installation has been completed.

Creating the Data Disk:

To Run The Program, A Student Data Disk Must Be Created On A Blank, Formatted, 3.5" Disk.

1. Click on **Start**, click on **Program**, then click on the **Goldrun (snowflake) icon**.
2. Insert a **blank, formatted, 3.5" disk** in drive A or B. At the Disk Drive Verification Form, select the disk drive (**drive A or B**) containing the blank, formatted disk.
3. At the **Create Data Disk** form press the Create Data Disk command button.
4. When the disk is completed press the **Continue** command button.
5. At the **Disk Drive Verification Form**, click on **Quit**.
6. Label your disk as GOLDRUN DATA. Include your name and the date. Before starting the program you may wish to make a backup copy of your data disk.

Begin The Program And Enter The Data!

When you have: **(1)** <u>carefully read pages 1-11</u>, **(2)** <u>a good understanding of the accounts</u> used by Gold Run Snowmobile, Incorporated, **(3)** <u>completed the installation of the program</u> as outlined on **page 14**, you are ready to begin the journalizing process.

The transactions for your first work week in December (4th through 10th) follow, and you are encouraged to prepare your account entry information before sitting down at the computer. This procedure will speed up your data entry time. An example of a written analysis for the first December 4 transaction is shown on **page 16**.

You may prefer to analyze each entry and record the transaction on the computer at the same time. You will be able to access the chart of accounts, customer list, and vendor list to the screen during the data entry process. This makes the recording of transactions and related information a very quick, easy, and efficient procedure.

TO BEGIN THE DATA ENTRY PROCESS, FOLLOW STEPS 1-5 AS OUTLINED BELOW:

1. *Insert the Data Disk in Drive A (or Drive B).*

2. *From the Task Bar Click on <u>Start</u>.*

3. *Click on Programs, then Click on the <u>GOLDRUN (snowflake) icon</u>.*

4. *Select Drive A (or Drive B), Wait for verification, and then Click on Continue.*

5. *On the first run of the program <u>You Must Enter Your Name</u> (see instructions below)!*

<u>**ENTER YOUR NAME**</u> and **check** it for **accuracy** (*it will be printed as entered on all documents*). Make any corrections necessary and then click on the <u>**OK - Save Name**</u> button. Your name is now encrypted on the data disk and all documents will be printed with your name and the date of the printing.

When the General Journal appears on the screen, click on the **Daily Entries** button. Read the narrative for the first December 4 transaction at the top of **page 16**. Carefully follow **instructions 1-6** as you begin the data entry procedure.

TRANSACTIONS FOR THE WEEK OF DECEMBER 4-10, 2001

Student Analysis

December 4
Performed service and adjustment work on a Swift Enduro Snowmobile and the customer paid cash for the work completed. The bill included $101.50 for 1.75 hours of labor ($58.00 per hour) plus sales tax (7%) of $7.11 (rounded to the nearest cent. The sales invoice number for this transaction is **G3006**. No parts were needed to complete this job.

101	108.61
411	101.50
205	7.11

This transaction has not been entered on the disk! Click on the Daily entries button and follow instructions 1-6 below.

1. *At the date prompt, for December 4, enter 04 for day and press the Enter key. When entering any part of the transaction, you may back up and reenter the information by using the backspace key. If the date has been entered incorrectly, click on the date prompt (DD) and reenter the date.*

2. *At the account prompt, type 101 and press the Enter or Tab key. To record the debit to Cash enter $108.61 in the debit amount column. Do not use dollar signs or commas. If the account or amount is incorrect, click on the appropriate item and reenter. Press the Enter or Tab key to move to the next position.*

3. *At the account prompt, type 411 and press the Enter or Tab key twice to move to the credit column. Enter $101.50 as the credit to Service Fees Earned and again press the Enter or Tab key.*

4. *Enter 205 to record the credit to Sales Tax Payable. Enter $7.11 as the credit amount and press the Tab (or Enter) key. When debits equal credits, the entry is complete. If any part of the journal entry is incorrect at this point, click on the Erase button and reenter the transaction.*

5. *At the invoice prompt enter G3006 as the sales invoice number. The alphabet letter G may be entered in upper or lower case.*

6. *Check the entry carefully. If you wish to make a correction to the invoice number, click on the invoice entry box and enter the correct number. If the entry is correct, click on the Post button.*

Continue entering the transactions for the first week. If you discover that a transaction entered into the system at an earlier time needs correction, **simply reverse or back out the incorrect entry and then enter the transaction correctly**. More detailed instructions on error correction procedures are on the next page. A complete summary of the error correction process is presented on **page 28**.

TRANSACTIONS FOR December 4-10, 2001

Student Analysis

December 4
Discovered that an entry of $19.75 for advertising printing charges had been recorded in error to the Miscellaneous Expense account rather than the Advertising Expense account. The date on the original cash transaction entry is *December 3* and the invoice number is **56789**.

1. *The entry correction procedure for the Gold Run Snowmobile accounting system requires that each error entry be backed out and then reentered correctly. Using the December 3 date, debit the Cash (101) account and credit the Miscellaneous Expense (635) account for the $19.75.*

2. *At the invoice prompt enter 56789 as the invoice number. When all of the data is correct, click on the Post button.*

3. *Since the date of the second entry is also December 3, click on the Repeat Date button above the date prompt or press D (for date) and the December 3 date will automatically be entered for you. This saves data entry time when several transactions are recorded on the same date.*

4. *Enter the transaction correctly with a debit to Advertising Expense (604) and a credit to Cash (101). When the check number prompt appears, enter ERROR to indicate that this is an error correction entry and a new check is not being issued.*

5. *Enter the 56789 invoice number as requested and when the data shown is correct, click on the Post button. Additional error correction instructions are found on page 28 of the student handbook.*

NOTE: *This error correction procedure leaves a clear audit trail of all corrections and is to be followed throughout this business simulation.*

NOTE: *If at any time you wish to view the journal entries that you have entered, click on the View Journal icon on the right side of the Tool Bar. Scroll through the journal entries or print a copy of the journal. Click on the Close button to return to the General Journal.*

TRANSACTIONS FOR THE WEEK OF DECEMBER 4-10, 2001

Student Analysis

Note: The following time-saving options may be used when journalizing transactions!

USING THE CHART OF ACCOUNTS FOR DATA ENTRY
AUTOMATIC BALANCING OF JOURNAL ENTRY AMOUNTS

December 4
Purchased on account from Buster Supply, store equipment listed at $386.00 and store supplies listed at $123.76. Sales taxes are included in the listed prices of these assets. The invoice number for this transaction is **B5667** and Buster Supply offers net 10 credit terms.

Enter the debit accounts and debit amounts. Enter the credit account and move to the credit amount column. Press the C key (for credit amount) at the dollar amount prompt and the correct credit amount will be automatically entered (debits will equal credits). For compound entries the credit amount of the last credited account can be entered automatically using the C key.

1. At the date prompt, enter 04 for the day.

2. Click on the <u>Chart</u> of Accounts button.

3. Click on account number 131, Store Equipment and Fixtures and the account name will automatically be entered in the account title column of the general journal. The account number will appear in the account number column. At the debit amount column enter $386.00.

4. Click on the <u>Chart</u> of Accounts button and then click on account number 127, Store and Shop Supplies. Enter the second debit amount of $123.76.

5. Click again on the Chart of Accounts button and then click on account number 201, Accounts Payable. Tab to the credit amount column, and <u>then press the C Key</u>. The correct balancing credit amount of <u>$509.76</u> will automatically be entered in the credit amount column. This feature may be used for both simple entries (one debit account and one credit account), and for compound journal entries at the last account credited.

6. At the invoice prompt enter B5667 as the invoice number.

7. At the vendor number prompt click on down arrow and select Buster Supply, the first vendor on the list. On future entries involving Accounts Payable or Accounts Receivable, use the scroll bar to select the correct vendor or customer.

8. When all of the data displayed is correct, click on the Post button and post the entry.

TRANSACTIONS FOR THE WEEK OF DECEMBER 4-10, 2001

Student Analysis

December 5
Sold for $7944.75 cash one model SW660 Swift Snowmobile. This model retails for $7425 plus 7% sales tax. The sales invoice for this transaction is **G3007**.

Because a perpetual inventory system is being used by Gold Run Snowmobile, Inc., for each entry where a product is being sold, an update of the specific inventory items being sold will be a part of the journalizing procedure. After each sale entry is posted, a second journal entry will automatically be entered and posted by the program. This entry will be a debit to the Cost of Goods Sold account and a credit to the Merchandise Inventory account.

1. *Enter the journal entry for the sales transaction. Follow with the sales invoice number and verify the transaction.*

2. *When the inventory information is requested by the program, enter the stock number of the item and the quantity sold.*

Merchandise listed on the sales invoice:

Stock Number	Item	Quantity	Net Cost Per Unit
SW660	**SWIFT ENDURO**	1	$5,940.00

NOTE: The snowmobile being sold for $7,425.00 cost the business $5,940.00 (net). All snowmobiles and snowmobile trailers carry a 25% markup on net cost (20% markup on selling price). The net cost ($5,940.00) plus the programmed markup of $1,485 ($5,940.00 x 25%) must equal the credit entry to sales ($7,425.00) or the journal entry will not be accepted.

When the Accumulated Sales total is in agreement with the credit to the Snowmobile, Accessories, & Parts Sales account, and all data is correct, click on the Post button.

When the sale and inventory entry has been entered, verified and posted, the system will automatically journalize and post to the Merchandise Inventory and the Cost of Goods Sold accounts.

TRANSACTIONS FOR THE WEEK OF DECEMBER 4-10, 2001

Student Analysis

December 5
Received a new shipment of Cruze Faceshields for inventory. **All merchandise purchases by Gold Run Snowmobile are recorded NET.** Invoice S4101 from Swift, Incorporated shows the list price of the merchandise at $150.00. Cash discount terms of 1/10, n/30 are offered and the merchandise is shipped FOB destination. *The calculated NET purchase price of the merchandise that will be recorded in the journal entry is $148.50 ($150.00 x .99).*

1. After entering the date, and the debit to Merchandise Inventory, click on the *Calculator* button.

2. The net price of the purchase can be calculated and entered in the journal directly from the calculator. Enter $150.00 (without a dollar sign or comma) on the calculator using the pointer and clicking on the numbers.

3. Click on the X sign (multiply) and then enter .99.

4. Click on the = sign. The correct net merchandise cost of $148.50 will be displayed.

5. Click on the Paste button on the bottom of the calculator and the net amount will automatically be entered in the debit amount column. The Paste procedure can be used at any time for a calculated amount.

6. Enter the appropriate credit entry, invoice number, and vendor number.

All completed invoice information will be displayed with the cost price of each merchandise item shown at the **NET PRICE** (list price less the purchase discount allowed). The **net cost price of the item purchased is shown below.**

Merchandise listed on the purchase invoice (at net cost):

Stock Number	Item	Quantity	Net Cost Per Unit
RR925	CRUZE FACESHIELD	15	$ 9.90

When the Accumulated Purchases total is in agreement with the debit to the Merchandise Inventory account the inventory entry is correct. Click on the Post button.

TRANSACTIONS FOR THE WEEK OF DECEMBER 4-10, 2001

Student Analysis

December 5
Issued check number **30091** to replenish the Petty Cash fund and to increase the size of the $50 fund to a $100 balance. Invoices for this transaction list $23.50 for store supplies, $16.75 for delivery charges, and $8.50 for miscellaneous items. There is currently $1.25 left in petty cash. At the invoice prompt enter **PCASH**.

Time-saving Entry Procedures To Remember:

1. *A click on the Repeat Date button will automatically enter date for you.*

2. *A click on the Chart button and the accounts can be entered with a single click.*

3. *All calculations can be made or verified with the Calculator. Entry amounts that are verified can be pasted directly to the journal debit or credit column.*

4. *THE LAST CREDIT AMOUNT ENTRIES can be entered by pressing the C key.*

∧∧∧

December 5
Received a check for $915 from the Downieville Dusters for storage fees on their snowmobiles and issued sales invoice number **G3008**. This check prepays their storage fees for December, January and February.

∧∧∧

December 6
Received a cash dividend of $.385 (38.5 cents) per share on the 1000 shares of Granite Corporation common stock held as a short-term investment. At the invoice prompt enter **CASHD** for cash dividend earned.

TRANSACTIONS FOR THE WEEK OF DECEMBER 4-10, 2001

Student Analysis

December 6
Received a new shipment of Trail-Tracker Snowmobiles for inventory. Invoice **T4357** from Trail-Tracker, Incorporated, lists the total **net purchase price of $27,244**, credit terms of 2/10, n/30, FOB destination shipping terms, and the models shipped.

Please note that all merchandise purchases by Gold Run Snowmobile are recorded NET.

The NET purchase price of the merchandise has been calculated at $27,244 (list price of $27,800 x .98 = total net cost of $27,244).

All completed invoice information will be displayed with the cost price of each merchandise item shown at the NET PRICE (list price less the purchase discount allowed). The net cost price of each item purchased is shown below.

Merchandise listed on the purchase invoice:

Stock Number	Item	Quantity	Net Cost Per Unit
T1500	TRAIL-TRACKER 1500	4	$4,116.00
T3000	TRAIL-TRACKER 3000	2	5,390.00

When the Accumulated Purchases total is in agreement with the debit to the Merchandise Inventory account, Click on the Post button.

TRANSACTIONS FOR THE WEEK OF DECEMBER 4-10, 2001

Student Analysis

December 6
Completed service and installation work on a customer snowmobile and the customer paid for the work in full. Sales invoice number **G3009** lists $116.00 for two hours of labor, $500.80 for accessories, and 7% sales tax on the total (labor and accessories). Round all sales tax calculations to the nearest cent (Example: $43.176= $43.18 sales tax).

Merchandise listed on the sales invoice:

Stock Number	Item	Quantity	Net Cost Per Unit
B4400	MUFFLER PAK	3	$65.30
CC555	SUPER DUTY SHOCK	2	27.25

Each muffler pak is being sold for $130.60 retail actually cost the business $65.30. The super duty shocks cost $27.25 each and are sold for $54.50. ALL accessories carry a 50% "normal" markup on selling price (100% markup on net cost).

∧∧∧

December 8
Billed the Running Ramblers $243.04 plus sales tax for accessories installed for no-charge on their team snowmobile (sales invoice number **G3010**).

Merchandise listed on the sales invoice:

Stock Number	Item	Quantity	Net Cost Per Unit
W1111	SPEEDOMETER	2	$29.40
W7777	TACHOMETER	2	31.36

TRANSACTIONS FOR THE WEEK OF DECEMBER 4-10, 2001

Student Analysis

December 8
The $842.00 account balance of customer Cathi Grobowski has proven to be uncollectible and is written off. Gold Run Snowmobile uses the allowance method for all bad debt write-offs. When the invoice number is requested type **WROFF**.

^^
December 8
Sold for cash **two** Trail-Tracker Enduro snowmobiles to customer Jasmin Rossette for $8,575.00 **each** plus sales tax (sales invoice number **G3011**).

Merchandise listed on the sales invoice:

Stock Number	Item	Quantity	Net Cost Per Unit
T3300	TRAIL-TRACKER ENDURO	2	$6,860.00

^^
December 9
Donated, to the Granite Bay High School Student Store, a cash register that is no longer being used. The cash register originally cost $770, has no current market value, and was fully depreciated two years ago. At the invoice prompt type **DONAT**.

TRANSACTIONS FOR THE WEEK OF DECEMBER 4-10, 2001

Student Analysis

December 9

Purchased merchandise on account from Swift Incorporated, at a total net cost of $62,172. The invoice number is **S4234**, cash terms are 1/10, n/30, and the merchandise is shipped FOB destination. Although a larger order was placed, due to heavy demand, only eight of the Swift Enduro snowmobiles were available for this shipment. Gold Run is currently out of stock on this very popular item.

Merchandise listed on the purchase invoice:

Stock Number	Item	Quantity	Net Cost Per Unit
SW660	SWIFT ENDURO	8	$5,940.00
SW999	SWIFT ARROW	1	9,900.00
SSS30	QUAD HAULER	4	1,188.00

∧∧∧

December 10

Purchased $5,010 worth of merchandise and accessories from Morelli Sports Equipment. The invoice number is **M4006**, cash terms are net 30, and the goods are shipped FOB shipping point. The transportation costs will be billed separately by the carrier.

Merchandise listed on the purchase invoice:

Stock Number	Item	Quantity	Net Cost Per Unit
J1001	M WIND TEK SUIT MD	14	$150.00
J2002	M WIND TEK SUIT LG	12	160.00
M0300	W TRAIL BOOTS	18	55.00

TRANSACTIONS FOR THE WEEK OF DECEMBER 4-10, 2001

Student Analysis

December 10
Issued check number **30092** and paid a cash dividend of $.23 per share to all December 1, stockholders of record. The dividend was declared on November 15, and is payable today, December 10. The company currently has 50,000 outstanding common shares. At the invoice prompt enter **DPAID** for dividend paid.

^^^

Now that you have completed entering the transactions for the first week of the internship program, December 4-10, it is time to check the accuracy of your work. In the **"Check It Out"** block on page **27** are the correct balances of key accounts that you have been working with this week.

1. Click on the **General Ledger** tab. The Trial Balance for December 9, 1999 will appear on the screen. Check your account balances against the correct totals shown in the **"Check It Out"** block on page **27**.

2. **IF ALL OF YOUR TOTALS MATCH THE CHECK FIGURES,** click on the merchandise **Inventory (*Red Snowmobile*)** button. The value of the perpetual inventory at the close of business on December 10 should total **$183,707.35**. This check figure should also match the Merchandise Inventory account balance found on the December 9 Trial Balance.

3. **If the inventory total also matches the check figure,** you may return to the General Journal and enter the transactions for December 10-16. However, if you wish to exit the program, click on **File** on the menu bar and click on **End Program**. Click on **Yes**, and **Exit** the program.

IF ANY OF YOUR BALANCES DO NOT MATCH THE CORRECT FIGURES, YOU HAVE ONE OR MORE ERRORS THAT MUST BE CORRECTED BEFORE YOU CAN CONTINUE. THE MOST EFFICIENT METHOD OF LOCATING AND CORRECTING THE ERROR/S is to print a copy of the general journal. Click on the **General Journal** tab and then click on the **View Journal** icon. Click on the **Print** icon and print a copy of the journal entries for the first week. If a printer is not available, you may view selected entries on the screen, however, this is a much more time-consuming process and is recommended **only** if a printer is not available. If you have several errors, you may also need to print a copy of the Trial Balance. Click on the **General Ledger** tab and the December 10, 2001 Trial Balance will appear on the screen. Click on the **Print** icon and print the document. Examine your documents, locate the error/s, and return to the General Journal and record the required correction entries.

> **"CHECK IT OUT"**
>
> | | |
> |---|---:|
> | 101 Cash | $ 41,599.39 |
> | 105 Accounts Receivable | 36,115.27 |
> | 106 Allowance for Doubtful Accounts | 107.50 |
> | 127 Store and Shop Supplies | 2,292.26 |
> | 132 Accumulated Depre., Store Equip. & Fix. | 14,430.00 |
> | 201 Accounts Payable | 137,962.26 |
> | 205 Sales Taxes Payable | 4,093.55 |
> | 207 Dividends Payable | 0.00 |
> | 221 Unearned Storage Fees | 11,015.00 |
> | 401 Snowmobile, Accessories, & Parts Sales | 162,968.84 |
> | 411 Service Fees Earned | 9,982.50 |
> | 501 Cost of Goods Sold | 100,131.92 |
> | 604 Advertising Expense | 1,734.75 |
> | 713 Dividends Earned | 504.00 |
> | TRIAL BALANCE | $682,503.60 |

Note carefully the proper error correction procedures that follow on page 26!

For **accuracy, efficiency,** and **a clear audit trail,** use **ONLY** the correction system designed for the Gold Run Snowmobile, Inc., accounting system. *Any account that is not correct is a MAJOR CLUE for you to check out.* If, for example, sales tax payable is one of the accounts that your total does not match, this is a strong indication that you have an error in one of the entries involving the sale of merchandise or services. This would include transactions of December 4, 5, 6 and 8. It could also indicate that sales tax was not charged correctly or possibly not charged at all in a sales transaction. An error, however, in the purchases account, would first require a close look at the entries of December 5, 6, 9, and 10.

PLEASE NOTE: Although no printed documents are required for December 10, if you wish any December 10 printouts, they must be printed BEFORE ENTRIES FOR THE SECOND ACCOUNTING PERIOD OF DECEMBER 11-17 ARE RECORDED. Additional entries will change the account balances. The Trial Balance and other statements for December 10 will not be stored for recall at a later time.

****

ERROR CORRECTION PROCEDURES
For the Gold Run Snowmobile Accounting System

JOURNAL ENTRY CORRECTION

Carefully examine all entries recorded for each period and when an error is found use the following correction procedure:

1. *Back the transaction out using the date used in the error entry.*

2. *Enter the correct transaction using the correct date of the original entry.*

If, for example, you find that a cash sales transaction for December 1 was entered without recording the sales tax, simply **back out (reverse)** the error as follows:

Dec. 1	Service Fees Earned	350.00	
	Cash		350.00

Enter **ERROR** at the check number prompt since this is a **correction** to cash and **does not** involve the issuance of another check. When the entry has been verified, the accounts will now show the original balances in place before the error entry.

Using the same Dec. 1 date, record the correct entry.

Dec. 1	Cash	378.00	
	Service Fees Earned		350.00
	Sales Tax Payable		28.00

The error entry, the backout entry, and the correction entry will appear in the accounting records leaving a clear, easy-to-follow audit trail.

When the account balances match those in the "Check It Out" block, you are ready to enter the transactions for the next period. If you are finished entering transactions for this session, return to the main menu and exit the system.

GOLD RUN SNOWMOBILE, INCORPORATED

TRANSACTIONS FOR DECEMBER 11-17

TRANSACTIONS FOR THE WEEK OF DECEMBER 11-17, 2001

Student Analysis

December 11
Sold old store equipment for $320 cash. The equipment originally cost $1,025 and depreciation to September 30 of this year (the end of the third quarter) totals $820. The asset depreciates on a straight-line basis at a rate of $20 per month and depreciation is calculated to the nearest month (two entries required). At the invoice prompt type **ASALE**.

∧∧∧

December 11
Issued check **30093** to the Oroville Freight Company for $199.75 as payment in full on invoice **L3111**. The invoice is for freight charges on merchandise *delivered to customers* under shipping terms of FOB destination.

∧∧∧

December 11
Returned shop supplies with a total cost of $56.00 to Buster Supply. The shop supplies were purchased on account December 4 (invoice number **B5667**).

∧∧∧

December 12
Received a certified check for **$1,310.00** from customer Alice Cordero as payment in full on her account. Ms. Cordero's account was written off as uncollectible on November 15 of this year (two entries required). At the invoice prompt type **RECOV**.

∧∧∧

December 12
Received a check from Western National Credit Card Company for $7,355.18 as payment in full on credit card invoices that had been received through December 3. The invoices, for sales made in late November and early December, totaled $7,641.75 and Western National charges a 3.75% fee for use of their system. The summary number for these invoices is **CC301**.

TRANSACTIONS FOR THE WEEK OF DECEMBER 11-17, 2001

Student Analysis

December 13
After exhausting all alternatives to initiate collection, wrote off the $435.00 balance of customer Chris Enburger. At the invoice prompt enter **WROFF**.

^^^

December 13
Purchased accessory items for inventory on credit from Fastwinn, Incorporated. The cash terms are 2/10, n/30, the purchase invoice number **44777**, and the goods are shipped FOB shipping point. Net purchase price for the merchandise is $573.30, added freight charges $43.50, and the final net amount of the invoice totals $616.80.

Merchandise listed on the purchase invoice:

Stock Number	Item	Quantity	Net Cost Per Unit
U1000	MICRO WINDSHIELD	5	$ 44.10
V0333	SNOWMOBILE COVER	6	58.80

Freight charges added to the invoice:

    Freight Charges $43.50

^^^

December 13
Instead of repairing the heavy duty shop hoist at a cost of $1,656 and charging this cost to an operating expense account, the hoist, which has one year remaining in its estimated useful life, is completely overhauled at a cost of $3,600 (check **30094**, invoice number **35556**). This overhaul will **extend the useful life** of the hoist to four years.

TRANSACTIONS FOR THE WEEK OF DECEMBER 11-17, 2001

Student Analysis

December 13
Sold **two** Trail-Tracker 2000 snowmobiles and a Norton trailer to customer Karen Osetto at an *out-the-door* price of $14,697.79 which **includes sales tax** (sales invoice number **G3012**). Ms. Osetto presented a check for $6,000 as a cash down payment and charged the balance to her account. The account will be paid in full in 30 days. To calculate the total sales amount divide the out-the-door price by 1.07. The difference between the answer and the total selling cost will be the sales tax.

Merchandise listed on the sales invoice:

Stock Number	Item	Quantity	Net Cost Per Unit
T2000	TRAIL-TRACKER 2000	2	$5,148.00
SD200	NORTON TRAILER DUO	1	693.00

∧∧∧

December 13
Issued a $370 check (**number 30095**) to Outdoors Unlimited magazine for advertising to be featured in the December 20 issue. Invoice number **87333** was received in today's mail.

∧∧∧

December 14
Sold six Swift snowmobiles and six batteries to the Colfax Sno Katts for $50,094 plus sales tax (sales invoice number **G3013**). The club presented a certified check as payment in full for their new equipment.

Merchandise listed on the sales invoice:

Stock Number	Item	Quantity	Net Cost Per Unit
SW660	SWIFT ENDURO	5	$5,940.00
SW999	SWIFT ARROW	1	9,900.00
A1150	SUPER CHARGER BATTERY	6	49.50

TRANSACTIONS FOR THE WEEK OF DECEMBER 11-17, 2001

Student Analysis

December 14
Issued check **30096** for as payment in full of the Buster Supply store equipment and store supplies purchase of December 4 (invoice number **B5667**), less the **$56.00 supply return** of December 11.

∧∧

December 15
Sold 500 shares of Ramblewood Manufacturing Corporation common stock that had been held as a short-term investment. The stock sold for 12 3/8, less a commission of $137.75. The stock was originally purchased as a block of 1,000 shares at a total cost (including commission) of $9,250.00. At the invoice prompt enter **STINV** for stock investment.

∧∧

December 15
Completed 3.25 hours of service and repair work and sold customer Mary Bermuda two snowmobile covers and four pairs of large snow mittens. Selling price of the merchandise is $414.40, labor is $58 per hour, plus sales tax on merchandise and labor (sales invoice number **G3014**). Mary charged the full amount to her account.

Merchandise listed on the sales invoice:

Stock Number	Item	Quantity	Net Cost Per Unit
V0333	SNOWMOBILE COVER	2	$58.80
LL355	SNOW MITTENS LARGE	4	22.40

∧∧

December 15
Received a check for $20,545 from Ruth Yates as payment in full on her account. The sales invoice number from this November 21 sale is **G2995**.

TRANSACTIONS FOR THE WEEK OF DECEMBER 11-17, 2001

Student Analysis

December 15
Issued check number **30097** to Zak Veedecampf, the part-time repair and sales person for the business. Zak is paid $8.50 per hour and worked 43.5 hours during the past two-week period ended December 14. At the invoice prompt enter **PAYRL**.

∧∧∧

December 15
Issued check number **30098** to Swift, Incorporated, as payment in full of invoice **S4101**. A total of fifteen Cruze faceshields were purchased for $148.50 (net) on December 5.

∧∧∧

December 16
Issued check **30099** in payment of invoice **T4357** from Trail-Tracker, Incorporated. Check the balance due to Trail-Tracker by calling up the Accounts Payable Subsidiary Ledger. Remember that this account balance has been recorded using the net method.

∧∧∧

December 16
Issued credit memo **CM307** to customer Mary Bermuda for $47.94 for the return of one pair of **LL355 SNOW MITTENS LARGE**. The mittens **sold** for $44.80 plus tax on December 15 (sales invoice number **G3014**). The inventory **cost** of the mittens is **$22.40**.

∧∧∧

December 17
Issued check **30100** to the Oroville Freight Company for $383.50 as payment in full on invoice **L3279**. The invoice is for freight charges on merchandise received from Morelli Sports Equipment on December 10.

TRANSACTIONS FOR THE WEEK OF DECEMBER 11-17, 2001

Student Analysis

December 17
Received notice from the bank that the $6,000 check received from customer Karen Osetto on December 13 has not cleared due to lack of funds. The balance of this NSF check and an additional $20 handling fee will be charged back to Ms. Osetto's account (sales invoice number **G3012**). The handling fee charged by Gold Run Snowmobile will be entered as Miscellaneous Revenue. At the check number prompt type **BADCK**.

∧∧∧

December 17
Completed 3.25 hours of service work and sold customer Alex Wong a Quad Hauler trailer. The retail selling price for the trailer is $1,485.00. The *full amount due*, including sales tax (sales invoice **G3015**), is paid with a <u>Bank Credit Card</u>. The bank will charge Gold Run Snowmobile a credit card fee (1-4%) which will be billed and recorded at the end of the month.

Merchandise listed on the sales invoice:

Stock Number	Item	Quantity	Net Cost Per Unit
SSS30	QUAD HAULER	1	$1,188.00

∧∧∧

December 17
Issued debit memo number **DM211** for $58.80 (net cost) and returned to Fastwinn, Incorporated, one **V0333 SNOWMOBILE COVER**. The cover contained a major defect in the side panel and was not saleable. It was part of a December 13 purchase (invoice **44777**).

When all of the transactions for the week of December 11-17 have been entered, Click on the General Ledger tab and the Trial Balance will appear on the screen. Carefully compare your totals to those in the **"Check It Out"** block. If any of the figures do not match the **"Check It Out"** block, you must carefully analyze all of your journal entries for the week, locate the error/s, and make the necessary corrections. To efficiently complete this analysis and correction procedure, it is recommended that you print a copy of the transactions you have entered. Click on the **General Journal** tab and then click on the **View Journal** icon. Select the journal entries for **December 11 to December 17** and print the documents. Be sure to use the **error correction procedures** outlined on **page 26** for **All** Error Corrections.

```
                    "CHECK IT OUT"

101 Cash ..................................... $ 99,801.29
105 Accounts Receivable ........................ 30,450.22
106 Allowance for Doubtful Accounts .............. 767.50
107 Accounts Rec., Credit Card Companies ......... 0.00
127 Store and Shop Supplies .................... 2,236.26
132 Accumulated Depre., Store Equip. & Fix.    13,610.00
136 Accumulated Depreciation, Shop Equipment   3,150.00
205 Sales Tax Payable .......................... 8,717.88
301 Common Stock ............................ 250,000.00
401 Snowmobile, Access., & Parts Sales ...    228,698.49
402 Sales Returns & Allowances ................ 1,561.80
411 Service Fees Earned ...................... 10,359.50
501 Cost of Goods Sold ...................... 152,390.72
505 Transportation-In ......................... 1,042.00
601 Salaries and Wages Expense .............. 17,384.75
604 Advertising Expense ...................... 2,104.75
607 Credit Card Expense ...................... 1,091.57
721 Gain on Sales of Assets .................... 155.00
731 Gain on Short-Term Investments ........... 1,424.75
TRIAL BALANCE ........................... $723,837.57
```

Click on the **General Ledger** tab and again on the **Inventory** (Red Snowmobile) button. The correct amount of perpetual inventory at the end of the December 17 work day should be **$131,963.05**. This total should match the balance of the Merchandise Inventory account on the December 17 Trial Balance.

PLEASE NOTE: ALL OF THE DECEMBER 17 DOCUMENTS MUST BE CORRECTED AND PRINTED BEFORE CONTINUING THE JOURNALIZING PROCESS IN WEEK THREE. THE DOCUMENTS ARE NOT STORED FOR LATER PRINTING. SINCE BALANCES ARE UPDATED AS NEW ENTRIES ARE RECORDED, DOCUMENTS FOR DECEMBER 17 CANNOT BE PRINTED IF ENTRIES AFTER DECEMBER 17 HAVE BEEN JOURNALIZED!

When your totals match the check figures, print the following documents:

1. Trial Balance for December 17, 2001

   Click on the General Ledger tab and print the Trial Balance.

2. Click on the Ledger Account icon and <u>print the Cash account that appears on the screen</u> (account 101).

   From the ledger selection box select and print the following <u>additional</u> General Ledger accounts:

   - 105 Accounts Receivable
   - 107 Accounts Receivable, Credit Card Companies
   - 115 Merchandise Inventory
   - 201 Accounts Payable
   - 401 Snowmobile, Accessories, & Parts Sales
   - 501 Cost of Goods Sold
   - 505 Transportation-In
   - 606 Delivery Expense

3. The Schedule of Accounts Receivable

   Click on the Subsidiary Ledgers tab. Click on the Print View icon and print the schedule.

4. The Individual account information for ALL customers

   Click on the Print All icon and print the Accounts Receivable Subsidiary Ledger.

5. The Schedule of Accounts Payable

   Click on the Accounts Payable View Schedule icon. Click on the Print View icon and print the schedule.

6. The Individual account information for ALL creditors/vendors

   Click on the Print All icon and print the Accounts Payable Subsidiary Ledger.

7. **The Inventory Analysis Form**

   Click on the General Ledger tab. Click on the Red Snowmobile and print the Inventory Analysis form.

8. **The Inventory Stock Cards for the following merchandise items:**

   Click on the Inventory Item icon and from the inventory selection box select and print the following inventory stock cards:

   SW660
   SSS30
   LL355
   V0333
   J1001
   RR925

To exit the program, click on **File** on the menu bar and click on **End Program**. Click on **Yes**, and **Exit** the program. Using your printed documents, carefully answer the questions on the **Mid-Project Evaluation** form.

PLEASE NOTE: ALL OF THE DECEMBER 17 DOCUMENTS MUST BE CORRECTED AND PRINTED BEFORE CONTINUING THE JOURNALIZING PROCESS IN WEEK THREE. THE DOCUMENTS ARE NOT STORED FOR LATER PRINTING. SINCE BALANCES ARE UPDATED AS NEW ENTRIES ARE RECORDED, DOCUMENTS FOR DECEMBER 17 CANNOT BE PRINTED IF ENTRIES AFTER DECEMBER 17 HAVE BEEN JOURNALIZED!

Using the printed documents, answer the questions on the Mid-Project Evaluation form. **BE SURE TO PRINT ALL OF YOUR DOCUMENTS BEFORE CONTINUING THE JOURNALIZING PROCESS FOR WEEK THREE!**

MID-PROJECT EVALUATION

GOLD RUN SNOWMOBILE, INC.

December 17, 2001

MID-PROJECT EVALUATION   NAME_____

GOLD RUN SNOWMOBILE, INC.   SECTION_____ DATE_____

1. Do the totals on your printed Trial Balance match the figures shown in the **"Check It Out"** block? YES_____ NO_____

2. What was the <u>correct balance</u> of the Cash account at the close of business on <u>December 5</u>? $_____

3. What invoice was paid in full with check number 30098 on December 15? Invoice Number_____

4. How many checks have been issued by the business during the period of December 4-11? _____

5. What is the current balance of the Buster Supply account? $_____

6. After the $56.00 return of supplies on December 11, what was the balance of the Buster Supply account? $_____

7. What was the balance of the Fastwinn, Incorporated, account after the purchase of merchandise on December 13? $_____

8. How much did the debit memo of December 17 reduce the balance owed to Fastwinn, Incorporated? $_____

9. What was the total (net) value of the merchandise purchased on account from Trail-Tracker, Inc., on December 6? $_____

10. If the Trail-Tracker, Inc., invoice (number T4357) had been filed on the wrong date and not paid on time, what would have been the cost for this error to Gold Run Snowmobile? $_____

11. Has the balance of accounts payable increased or decreased since December 3? _____

12. Assuming that all discounts offered are taken, on what date is the balance owed to Swift, Incorporated due and payable? Date_____

13. Assuming the Swift, Incorporated invoice is not paid on time as intended, what will be the total amount of the discount lost? $_____

14. On what date is the November 26 invoice from Butler & Kadnaso due and payable? Date_____

15. Due to a filing error the balance of one vendor's account has passed the discount period and the discount has been lost (the entry will be recorded later). How much will this error cost Gold Run Snowmobile? $_____

16-17. From December 4 to 17 there were several purchases of merchandise. From which vendor was the largest purchase made and what was the amount of the purchase? Vendor Number_____ $_____

MID PROJECT EVALUATION
GOLD RUN SNOWMOBILE, INC.

18-19. Which customer paid invoice number G2995 in full and on what date was the invoice paid?
    Customer Number_____
    Date_____

20. Does the balance of the Schedule of Accounts Receivable match the balance of the Accounts Receivable account?
    YES_____ NO_____

21. What is the balance of Mary Bermuda's account?
    $_____

22. How did Cathi Grobowski's account balance get reduced to zero?
    _____

23. How many customer accounts have had no activity during December?
    _____

24. Has the balance of accounts receivable increased or decreased since December 3?
    _____

25. What was the total amount of Snowmobile, Accessories, and Parts Sales for the period of December 8-13?
    $_____

26. If a freight invoice is received and charges listed are for shipments of merchandise to Gold Run Snowmobile customers, what account will be debited for this billing?
    _____

27. What is the General Ledger account classification of the Dividends Declared account?
    _____

28. How many inventory items are at or below the "reorder point"?
    _____

29. How many inventory items are currently "out of stock"?
    _____

30. How many T3000 Snowmobiles are currently on hand?
    _____

31. Should a purchase order be sent to Trail-Tracker, Inc., for additional inventory of snowmobiles?
    YES_____ NO_____

32. What is the inventory stock number for a Neon Cap?
    Stock Number_____

33. To what inventory item has stock number U0001 been assigned?
    _____

34. How many units of stock number V0333 were returned to the vendor on December 17?
    _____

35. How many units of stock number SW660 have been sold since December 3?
    _____

36. What is the current FIFO inventory value of all units of stock number SW660?
    $_____

37. What is the current FIFO inventory value of all units of stock number RR925?
    $_____

MID PROJECT EVALUATION
GOLD RUN SNOWMOBILE, INC.

38. How many units below the reorder point is the inventory for U0012? _____

39-40. How many SSS30 Quad Hauler Trailers were purchased on December 9 and what was the cost per unit? _____

Unit Cost $_____

41. How many cases of Cruze oil are currently on hand? _____

42. All snowmobiles and snowmobile trailers carry a markup on cost of 25% (markup on selling price of 20%). What should be the retail selling price of a Norton Trailer Duo, inventory number SD200? $_____

43. If markup on selling price is 20%, what will be the retail selling price of item T2000, a Trail Tracker 2000 snowmobile? $_____

Answer questions 44-50 using the balances at the close of business activity, December 17.

44. What is the total for **Net** Snowmobile, Accessories, and Parts Sales? $_____

45. What is the **Net** value of Accounts Receivable? $_____

46. What is the balance owed to Gold Run Snowmobile, Inc., by credit card companies? $_____

47. As of December 17, how much will the freight costs for the purchase of merchandise inventory add to the Cost of Goods Sold? $_____

48. How many dollars worth of merchandise (at retail) have been returned by customers since December 3 (see appendix)? $_____

49. How much has it cost Gold Run Snowmobile, Inc., to send merchandise to customers? $_____

50. Check number 30094 was issued for $3,600 on December 13 as payment in full of invoice 35556. Was this expenditure a" normal repair, extraordinary repair, or a betterment? _____

GOLD RUN SNOWMOBILE, INCORPORATED

TRANSACTIONS FOR DECEMBER 18-24

TRANSACTIONS FOR THE WEEK OF DECEMBER 18-24, 2001

Student Analysis

December 18
Issued check number **30101** for $214.00 to Loomis Repair Service for emergency repairs on the shop equipment (invoice **LR554**).

∧∧

December 18
Discovered that invoice **N3302** from Norton America for $15,900 list (**$15,741 net**), with cash terms of 1/10, n/30, and dated November 18, was filed incorrectly and the cash discount has been lost. **Record the discount lost entry.** Then issue check number **30102** and pay the total amount due today on this invoice. **Two separate entries must be entered to properly record this transaction.**

∧∧

December 18
Received a $1,100 check from the Downieville Dusters as a partial payment on their past due account (**G2768**).

∧∧

December 18
On October 19 of this year Gold Run Snowmobile, Inc., borrowed cash by discounting a $11,000, 60-day, note payable. The lender charged Gold Run Snowmobile a 12% discount fee and the Interest Expense account was debited for $220. Proceeds of $10,780 were received and deposited in the Cash account. This $11,000 note **due today** and is **paid in full** with check number **30103**. At the invoice prompt enter **NTPAY**.

TRANSACTIONS FOR THE WEEK OF DECEMBER 18-24, 2001

Student Analysis

December 19
Sold one Trail-Tracker Enduro snowmobile to A. C. Woolworth for the cost of $6,860 **plus a markup on selling price of 20%**. Sales tax on the retail price increases the out-the-door *cash* price to $9,175.25. The sales invoice number for this transaction is G3016.

Merchandise listed on the sales invoice:

Stock Number	Item	Quantity	Net Cost Per Unit
T3300	TRAIL-TRACKER ENDURO	1	$6,860.00

∧∧∧

December 19
Issued check number **30104** to Swift Incorporated as payment in full for invoice S4234 of December 9. Check the accounting records to determine the exact amount of the invoice.

∧∧∧

December 19
Sold a quad trailer and accessory items to the Mt. Shasta Snowmobile Club and received a club check for the balance due. Sales invoice number **G3017**, lists the merchandise items at $7,841.00 and 7% sales tax totaling $548.87.

Merchandise listed on the sales invoice:

Stock Number	Item	Quantity	Net Cost Per Unit
B3000	CUSTOM DECAL KIT	5	$32.00
RR404	CRUZE HELMET	6	65.50
RR555	DELUXE RACING HELMET	12	95.00
SSS30	QUAD HAULER	3	1,188.00

TRANSACTIONS FOR THE WEEK OF DECEMBER 18-24, 2001

Student Analysis

On the following purchase invoice, one of the items purchased has a new cost price that must be entered in the inventory records <u>before the journal entry can be recorded</u>.

1. Click on the General Ledger tab.

2. Click on the Red Snowmobile icon.

3. When the Inventory Analysis form appears on the screen, click on the White Snowmobile (Change Price) icon.

4. Enter inventory stock number <u>SSS30</u> and the current cost of <u>$1,188.00 per unit will appear on the screen</u>. Enter the new cost price of <u>$1,287.00</u> per unit.

5. Click on the Save Change button, then click on the Close Form button.

6. Click on the Close Form icon to exit the Inventory Analysis section.

7. Click on the General Journal tab and then click on the Daily Entries button. Enter the December 20 purchase from Swift Arrow.

December 20
Purchased a special order Swift Arrow and three additional Quad Hauler trailers from Swift, Incorporated. The gross invoice total from Swift, Inc. (including freight charges), is $14,071. **The total net cost of the merchandise is $13,761 with an additional freight charge of $310.** The terms on invoice S4385 are 1/10, n/30 and the special order is being shipped FOB shipping point. The net cost of this popular trailer has increased from $1,188 to $1,287 since the last order.

Merchandise listed on the purchase invoice:

Stock Number	Item	Quantity	Net Cost Per Unit
SW999	SWIFT ARROW	1	$9,900.00
SSS30	QUAD HAULER	3	1,287.00

Freight charges added to the invoice:

Freight Charges	$310.00

TRANSACTIONS FOR THE WEEK OF DECEMBER 18-24, 2001

Student Analysis

December 20
Received a check for $1,350.00 from the Colfax Sno Katts as payment for six months rent (January-June) on their club's storage space. The sales invoice for this transaction is **G3018**.

∧∧∧

December 21
Issued check **30105** for $135.00 to the Highlander Freight Company (invoice **H3200**) for charges on the shipment of merchandise items to the Mt. Shasta Snowmobile Club.

∧∧∧

December 21
Repaired a damaged steering mechanism for customer Ruth Yates. Ruth was billed for 1.75 hours of labor ($58 per hour), accessories totaling $70, plus sales tax (sales invoice number **G3019**). Ruth charged this repair to her account.

Merchandise listed on the sales invoice:

Stock Number	Item	Quantity	Net Cost Per Unit
CC100	STANDARD SHOCK	2	$ 17.50

∧∧∧

December 21
Purchased accessories with a total cost of $1,185 from Morelli Sports Equipment. The merchandise was delivered by Morelli (invoice number **M4577**, terms net 30.)

Merchandise listed on the purchase invoice:

Stock Number	Item	Quantity	Net Cost Per Unit
LL466	COMPETITION GLOVES	15	$ 79.00

TRANSACTIONS FOR THE WEEK OF DECEMBER 18-24, 2001

Student Analysis

December 22
Traded the old company truck for a new truck issuing check number **30106** to complete the transaction. The old used truck cost $3,800 and on September 30, the end of the quarter, had depreciated $2,200. Straight-line depreciation on the old truck is $40 per month. The new truck listed (invoice **R2567**) for $19,950 (taxes and destination charges included), and Auburn Auto Sales allowed a $3,000 trade-in allowance on the purchase of the new vehicle. An additional check (number **30107**) for $540 was issued to the Department of Motor Vehicles (invoice **DMV12**) for the vehicle license fees. Three entries are required for this trade.

∧∧∧

December 22
Issued check **30108** in payment of the purchase invoice (**44777**) from Fastwinn, Inc. Check the purchase invoice of **December 13** and the merchandise return of **December 17** for more detailed information on this obligation.

∧∧∧

December 23
Issued check **30109** and purchased additional store fixtures for better display and security of merchandise. The equipment lists for $4,200, with **trade discounts of 40% and 10%,** and sales tax on the net amount. The invoice number for this purchase is **X5001**.

∧∧∧

December 23
Purchased additional store and shop supplies on account from Buster Supply. Invoice **B6016** lists credit terms of net 10 and a balance due of $385.50.

TRANSACTIONS FOR THE WEEK OF DECEMBER 18-24, 2001

Student Analysis

December 23
Sold the special order Swift Arrow snowmobile and a Quad Hauler trailer to customers Jason and Kristin Turner. Sales invoice number **G3020** shows the total sales price including tax to be $14,990.00. The Turners paid $4,990.00 as a cash down payment and Gold Run accepted a short-term, $10,000, 14%, 90-day note receivable for the balance. To calculate the amount of the sale (before sales tax) divide the total sales price by 1.07.

Merchandise listed on the sales invoice:

Stock Number	Item	Quantity	Net Cost Per Unit
SW999	SWIFT ARROW	1	$9,900.00
SSS30	QUAD HAULER	1	1,287.00
EE222	FUEL TANK 6 GALLON	2	6.40

∧∧

December 23
Sold accessories for $152.00 plus sales tax (sales invoice number **G3021**). The customer, Alice Cordero charged the entire amount to her account.

Merchandise listed on the sales invoice:

Stock Number	Item	Quantity	Net Cost Per Unit
B7777	LUGGAGE CARRIER	2	$ 38.00

TRANSACTIONS FOR THE WEEK OF DECEMBER 18-24, 2001

Student Analysis

December 24
Returned accessories costing $158.00 that were purchased on December 21 from Morelli Sports Equipment (debit memo **DM212**). The original invoice number was **M4577**.

Items returned with the debit memo:

Stock Number	Item	Quantity	Net Cost Per Unit
LL466	COMPETITION GLOVES	2	$ 79.00

∧∧

December 24
Sold two Trail-Tracker 1500 snowmobiles and a Norton Duo trailer at an out-the-door price of $11,937.19 (**sales tax included**). The customer paid using a <u>Bank Credit Card</u>. The sales invoice number is **G3022**.

Merchandise listed on the sales invoice:

Stock Number	Item	Quantity	Net Cost Per Unit
T1500	TRAILER-TRACKER 1500	2	$4,116.00
SD200	NORTON DUO TRAILER	1	693.00

∧∧

December 24
Sold a used piece of shop equipment for $1,995. The equipment was purchased at a total cost of $7,200 early in 1998. Using **units of production depreciation**, the accumulated depreciation account balance at the end of the third quarter (September 30, 2001) totals $2,850. Depreciation is recorded at the rate of $2.00 for each hour of operation. To December 24 of this quarter, an additional 234 hours of operation have accumulated on the hour meter. **Two entries are required to properly record this sale.** At the invoice prompt enter **ASALE** for asset sale.

TRANSACTIONS FOR THE WEEK OF DECEMBER 18-24, 2001

Student Analysis

December 24
Received payment in full on a $9,600, 10%, 60-day note receivable from customer Alfred Moss. The note, dated October 25, matures today. Enter **NTREC** (for note receivable) at the invoice prompt. For all interest calculations be sure to use the 360-day banker's year.

^^

When all of the transactions for the week have been entered, click on the **General Ledger** tab bring the trial balance to the screen. Check your account totals against the figures in the **"Check It Out"** block. Click on the **Inventory** (red snowmobile) button and check the perpetual inventory total. The correct value of the *perpetual inventory* is **$114,398.25**. If all of your totals match the check figures, you are ready to enter the transactions for the week of December 26-31. If your totals do not match the check figures, carefully check the journal entries, locate the error/s, and enter the necessary correction/s.

"CHECK IT OUT"

101 Cash	$ 38,602.84
105 Accounts Receivable	29,696.37
109 Notes Receivable	10,000.00
127 Store and Shop Supplies	2,621.76
131 Store Equipment and Fixtures	52,717.76
140 Accumulated Depreciation, Trucks	4,550.00
201 Accounts Payable	47,630.50
205 Sales Tax Payable	11,651.24
401 Snowmobile, Accessories, & Parts Sales	270,502.09
501 Cost of Goods Sold	184,743.52
505 Transportation-In	1,352.00
603 Truck & Equipment Operating Expense	1,026.95
606 Delivery Expense	886.50
607 Credit Card Expense	1,091.57
612 Depreciation Expense, Trucks	120.00
628 License Expense	856.00
633 Discounts Lost	193.00
711 Interest Earned	472.00
721 Gain on Sale of Assets	155.00
813 Interest Expense	319.00
821 Loss on Sale/Disposal of Assets	1,887.00
TRIAL BALANCE	$691,148.53

GOLD RUN SNOWMOBILE, INCORPORATED

TRANSACTIONS FOR DECEMBER 26-31

TRANSACTIONS FOR THE WEEK OF DECEMBER 26-31, 2001

Student Analysis

December 26
Issued the following checks as payment in full for miscellaneous billings:

Check **30110** for $423.50 to Cuppinger and Company Accountancy for accounting services received (invoice **K2146**).

Check **30111** for $975.00 to Blu and Delery Insurance Agency for additional coverage on the new storage areas (invoice **B7676**).

Check **30112** to Mountain Rider magazine for advertising to be featured in current and future issues. The invoice balance is for $1,550.00 (invoice **32000**).

Check **30113** to Sierra Truck Service for gas and truck repairs totaling $254.25 (invoice **44555**).

^^
December 26
Received a new shipment of Trail-Tracker snowmobiles and accessories for inventory. Invoice **T4587** from Trail-Tracker presents the total **LIST PRICE** of this purchase for $33,600, credit terms of 2/10, n/30, and FOB destination shipping terms. Remember that all merchandise purchases are recorded **NET**.

Merchandise listed on the purchase invoice:

Stock Number	Item	Quantity	Cost Per Unit
T1500	TRAIL-TRACKER 1500	8	$4,116.00

TRANSACTIONS FOR THE WEEK OF DECEMBER 26-31, 2001

Student Analysis

December 26
Purchased for a special order, eight Solo model trailers from Fastwinn, Incorporated. Credit terms offered are 2/10, n/30, and the trailers for this special order are delivered by Fastwinn. The invoice number is **45801** and the total **LIST PRICE** of this purchase is $4,000.

Merchandise listed on the purchase invoice:

Stock Number	Item	Quantity	Cost Per Unit
SS100	NORTON TRAILER SOLO	8	$490.00

∧∧

December 26
Issued check **30114** to Butler & Kadnaso as payment in full on invoice **21777** of November 26. Check your copy of the December 17 subsidiary ledger or click on the Subsidiary Ledger tab and then the Butler & Kadnaso account to determine the amount due.

∧∧

December 26
Borrowed an additional $30,000 cash by issuing a 60-day discounted note payable to a private lender. The lender charges a **12%** discount fee. Proceeds from this note total $29,400. Because of the timing of this note, the lender discount will be debited to the Discount on Notes Payable account. At the invoice prompt enter **DISNT** for discounted note.

∧∧

December 26
Issued check **30115** to the State Board of Equalization for the balance of the sales tax collected through the close of the work day on December 24. The "Check It Out" box at the end of week three week lists the correct balance of this account on December 24. At the invoice prompt enter **SALTX** for sales tax.

TRANSACTIONS FOR THE WEEK OF DECEMBER 26-31, 2001

Student Analysis

December 26
Received a check for $5,712.22 from Ray Norburg as payment in full on his account. Mr. Norburg purchased a new Trail-Tracker snowmobile and accessories on November 26 (sales invoice number **G2999**).

∧∧∧

On the following purchase invoice, one of the items purchased has a new cost price that must be entered in the inventory records <u>before the journal entry can be recorded</u>.

1. Click on the General Ledger tab.

2. Click on the Red Snowmobile icon.

3. When the Inventory Analysis form appears on the screen, click on the White Snowmobile (Change Price) icon.

4. Enter inventory stock number <u>Z9000</u> and the current cost of <u>$22.00 per</u> unit will appear <u>on the screen</u>. Enter the new cost price of <u>$25.00</u> per unit.

5. Click on the Save Change button, then click on the Close Form button.

6. Click on the Close Form icon to exit the Inventory Analysis section.

7. Click on the General Journal tab and then click on the Daily Entries button. Enter the December 27 purchase from Trail-Tracker.

December 27
Received a second shipment of Trail-Tracker snowmobiles and accessories for inventory. Invoice **T4608** from Trail-Tracker lists the total **net purchase** of $52,011, credit terms of 2/10, n/30, and FOB destination shipping terms.

Merchandise listed on the purchase invoice:

Stock Number	Item	Quantity	Net Cost Per Unit
T2000	TRAIL-TRACKER 2000	10	$5,148.00
Z9000	TEAM TR-TRACKER BAG	6	25.00
ZZ100	TRAIL-TRACKER JACKET	6	63.50

TRANSACTIONS FOR THE WEEK OF DECEMBER 26-31, 2001

Student Analysis

December 27
Purchased on account accessory items for inventory from Fastwinn, Incorporated. The credit terms are 2/10, n/30, the purchase invoice number **45905**, and the goods are shipped FOB shipping point. Total **net** purchase price for the merchandise is $820.00, and added freight charges listed on the invoice total $67.00.

Merchandise listed on the purchase invoice:

Stock Number	Item	Quantity	Cost Per Unit
XX333	HOTSHOT OIL CASE	20	$32.00
V4400	SADDLE BAGS	5	36.00

Freight charges added to the invoice:

Freight Charges	**$67.00**

^^

December 28
Through a telephone order, sold two Trail-Tracker snowmobiles at an out-the-door selling price (including tax) of $11,010.30. The customer, from Goose Lake, paid for the snowmobiles with a **Western National credit card**. The sales invoice number is **G3023**.

Merchandise listed on the purchase invoice:

Stock Number	Item	Quantity	Cost Per Unit
T1500	TRAIL-TRACKER 1500	2	$4,116.00

^^

December 28
Shipped the two Trail-Tracker snowmobiles sold to the Goose Lake phone customer. Charged the $67.50 freight costs to our account with Inglass Incorporated, a local carrier, (invoice number **C3112**).

TRANSACTIONS FOR THE WEEK OF DECEMBER 26-31, 2001

Student Analysis

December 28
Recorded a major sale (sales invoice **G3024**) to the Eagle Mountain Snowmobile Club. Received a $25,000, 14%, 60-day note receivable (dated today) and the remaining balance in cash. Calculate the total amount of the sale (including 7% sales tax of $3,894.98). Remember that all snowmobiles are sold with a **25%** markup on cost.

Merchandise listed on the sales invoice:

Stock Number	Item	Quantity	Cost Per Unit
SW660	SWIFT ENDURO	2	$5,940.00
T1500	TRAIL-TRACKER 1500	4	4,116.00
T3000	TRAIL-TRACKER 3000	3	5,390.00

^^

December 28
Customer Pete Peterson paid $201.70 (sales tax included) for 3.25 hours of service work on his snowmobile. Pete paid in full using his <u>Bank Credit Card</u>. The sales invoice for this transaction is **G3025**.

^^

December 29
Received a check for $1,110 from the Sierra College Snowmobile Club for storage fees on their club equipment (sales invoice **G3026**). The check covers the storage fees for six months beginning January 1, 2002.

TRANSACTIONS FOR THE WEEK OF DECEMBER 26-31, 2001

Student Analysis

December 29
Sold two fanny paks and two neon caps to customer Doug Winchester for $93.00 and also charged Mr. Winchester for 1.75 hours of additional service work on his snowmobile (be sure to include sales tax). The sales invoice number is **G3027** and Mr. Winchester paid cash for his merchandise and service work.

Merchandise listed on the sales invoice:

Stock Number	Item	Quantity	Cost Per Unit
U2200	FANNY PAK	2	$17.25
N6000	NEON CAP	2	6.00

∧∧∧

December 30
Issued check **30116** to Swift Incorporated as payment in full on invoice **S4385** of December 20. If paid on time, the net balance due is $14,071.

∧∧∧

December 30
Issued check **30117** for $18,500 to Jan-Lyn Electric of Gold Run for leasehold improvements made to the hoist and storage areas. The invoice number from Jan-lyn is **JL555**.

∧∧∧

December 30
Issued check **30118** for $12.84 to customer Doug Winchester as a cash refund for the neon cap he returned (stock number **N6000** with a cost of **$6.00**). The check is for a $12.00 merchandise return plus sales tax. The original sales invoice number was **G3027** and the credit memo number is **CM308**.

TRANSACTIONS FOR THE WEEK OF DECEMBER 26-31, 2001

Student Analysis

December 30
Issued check **30119** for $54.10 to replenish the Petty Cash Fund. A total of **$45.90** remains in the petty cash box at this time. Be sure to account for the cash overage or shortage. At the invoice prompt enter **PCASH**. A summary of receipts shows the following expenditures have been made to date from Petty Cash:

> Store & Shop Supplies $ 35.10
> Tools Expense   11.50
> Miscellaneous Expense   6.50

^^

December 30
Issued check number **30120** to Zachary Veedcampf, the part-time employee. Zachary is paid $8.50 per hour and worked **34 hours** during the past two-week pay period ended December 28. At the invoice prompt enter **PAYRL**.

^^

December 31
Issued check number **30121** to Acme Tools for the $53.45 cash purchase of miscellaneous tools to be used in the service shop. The invoice for this purchase is number **76611**.

^^

December 31
Sold for **9 3/4** the remaining 500 shares of the Ramblewood Manufacturing Corporation common stock that was held as a short-term investment. The commission charge was $126.00. This stock was a part of a block of 1,000 shares purchased earlier at a total cost of $9,250.00. At the invoice prompt enter **INVST**.

^^

When all of the transactions for the week of December 26-31 have been entered, click on the **General Ledger** tab and the December 31, 2001 Trial Balance will appear on the screen. Carefully compare your totals to those in the "Check It Out" block on page **65**. If any of the figures do not match the "Check It Out" block, you **must carefully analyze**

all of your journal entries for the period, locate the error/s, and make the necessary corrections. To efficiently complete this analysis and correction procedure, click on print icon and print a copy of the Trial Balance. Then click on the **General Journal** tab and print the journal entries for **December 26 to 31**. Be sure to use the **error correction procedures** outlined on **page 28** for **All** Error Corrections.

When your Trial Balance totals match the check figures, click on the **Inventory** button and check that your perpetual inventory total for December 31 totals **$151,290.75**. This perpetual total should also match the balance of the Merchandise Inventory account as shown on the December 31, Trial Balance.

When all of your totals match the check figures, you are ready to proceed to the December 31, 2001 bank reconciliation.

"CHECK IT OUT"

101 Cash	$ 51,891.98
105 Accounts Receivable	23,984.15
107 Accounts Rec., Credit Card Companies	11,010.30
109 Notes Receivable	35,000.00
127 Store and Shop Supplies	2,656.86
136 Accumulated Depreciation, Shop Equipment	300.00
145 Leasehold Improvements	18,500.00
201 Accounts Payable	108,578.00
203 Notes Payable	32,000.00
204 Discount On Notes Payable	600.00
205 Sales Tax Payable	4,641.26
221 Unearned Storage Fees	13,475.00
401 Snowmobile, Accessories, & Parts Sales	336,527.59
402 Sales Returns and Allowances	1,573.80
411 Service Fees Earned	10,751.00
501 Cost of Goods Sold	237,530.02
505 Transportation-In	1,419.00
604 Advertising Expense	3,654.75
606 Delivery Expense	954.00
607 Credit Card Expense	1,091.57
631 Cash Short & Over	17.00
711 Interest Earned	472.00
731 Gain on Short-Term Investments	1,548.75
TRIAL BALANCE	**$ 842,635.55**

BANK RECONCILIATION

Before entering your adjusting entries, complete the bank reconciliation (page 69) for December 31, 2001, the statement date and the last workday of the month. *Enter the cash balance from the trial balance as the book balance* and **$48,388.77** as the **bank statement balance**. Additional information needed to complete the reconciliation is listed below:

1. A late deposit of **$4,749.00** was not listed on the bank statement.

2. Accrued interest earned on the checking account totals **$79.56**.

3. The debit memo from the bank for miscellaneous account services (charged to Bank Service Charges) totals **$32.17**.

4. During the month of June, customers purchased **$13,929.54** in merchandise and services using their **bank credit cards**. A debit memo with the bank statement charges Gold Run Snowmobile 3% of the total of these sales receipts as a credit card fee (Credit Card Expense). On all calculations remember to round your answer to the nearest cent.

5. Checks **30112, 30118,** and **30121** were not returned with the bank statement.

Using the **Journalize Daily Entries** option, record the required transactions resulting from the bank reconciliation. Since the entries are **updating** the balance of the cash account and **no check is being issued**, when the system asks for a check number, enter **BKS12**. When an invoice number is requested for the interest earned, or bank service charge, also enter **BKS12** (Bank Statement for December).

* *
Student Analysis

Print a copy of the Trial Balance! **THIS IS THE TRIAL BALANCE THAT WILL BE USED WHEN RECORDING THE ADJUSTING ENTRIES FOR THE BUSINESS!** The new December 31, 2001 Trial Balance check figure is **$842,715.11**. The new balance of the **Cash** account is **$51,521.48**, **Miscellaneous Expense** is unchanged at **$86.75**, **Interest Earned** totals **$551.56**, and **Credit Card Expense** totals **$1,509.46**. If your balances match these figures, you are ready to record the adjusting entries.

BANK RECONCILIATION   NAME_____

GOLD RUN SNOWMOBILE, INC.   SECTION_____ DATE_____

BANK RECONCILIATION
GOLD RUN SNOWMOBILE, INCORPORATED
DECEMBER 31, 2001

Book Balance: $_____

    Add:

    _____   _____

Total $_____

    Deduct:

_____ $_____

_____ _____ $_____

Reconciled Book Balance $_____
                                                                 ==========

Bank Balance: $_____

    Add:

    _____   _____

Total $_____

    Deduct:

    _____

        Check No. _____ $_____
        Check No. _____   _____
        Check No. _____   _____ $_____

Reconciled Bank Balance $_____
                                                                 ==========

GOLD RUN SNOWMOBILE

ADJUSTING AND CLOSING ENTRIES

For the Quarter Ended December 31, 2001

ADJUSTING ENTRIES FOR THE QUARTER

Using a copy of the December 31 Unadjusted Trial Balance (printed after the bank reconciliation entries) and the information and financial data shown below, record the adjusting entries for Gold Run Snowmobile, Inc. **Be sure to click on the ADJUSTING entries button** on the tool bar. Adjusting entries **must not** be entered using the **Daily entries** procedure. Any corrections to adjusting entries must also be entered using the **Adjusting entries option**. Adjusting entries **will not** require documentation entries. Where necessary in the calculations, round all totals to the nearest cent. **ALL ENTRIES MUST BE RECORDED AS OF DECEMBER 31, 2001, THE END OF THE FOURTH QUARTER!**

A. The **unexpired** insurance balance is **$3,530**.

B. The ending store and shop supplies inventory is **$1,231.55**.

C. A total of **$950** worth of advertising copy, paid for and **correctly charged** to the Advertising Expense account, will be received early next quarter.

D. All of the prepaid property tax is an expense for the quarter.

E. Wages accrued total **12 hours** worked at **$8.50 per hour**.

F. Straight-line depreciation of store equipment and fixtures totals **$2,125 for the quarter**.

G. Depreciation of shop equipment is **$560 for the quarter**.

H. Gold Run Snowmobile, Inc., has three trucks. The new truck acquired on December 22 will not depreciate this quarter. An old truck used only for short distance heavy hauling is fully depreciated. The third truck was acquired at a cost of $25,000, has a salvage value of $7,000, is depreciated on a miles driven basis (**units of production depreciation**), and has an estimated service life of 100,000 miles. The truck was driven **3,212 miles** during the fourth quarter.

I. Accrue the interest on the **short-term** notes receivable. **Calculate the interest on each note to the nearest cent. Use the 360-day banker's year for all interest computations.**

Note One: $10,000, 14%, 90-day note, dated December 23

Note Two: $25,000, 14%, 60-day note, dated December 28

J. Recognize the interest on the **short-term** note payable. On December 26, **$30,000** was borrowed for **60 days** on a **discounted basis** (discount rate **12.0%**) and $600 was debited to the Discount on Notes Payable account.

K. Storage Fees Earned for the quarter total **$9,360**.

L. Additional income taxes expense for the period total **$2,001**.

M. Amortize the **quarterly** portion of the Leasehold account to Rent Expense. As of September 30, the end of the third quarter, **exactly four years** remain on the lease agreement.

N Amortize $125 of the Discount on Lease Financing account balance to the Interest Expense account.

O. The balance sheet (computer aging) method is used to estimate the Bad Debt Expense and the balance of the Allowance for Doubtful Accounts account for the end of each quarter. The program has analyzed all accounts receivable and calculated the estimated balance of the Allowance for Doubtful Accounts balance to be **$1,420.50**.

P. Credit Card Expense (**3.75%**) on the outstanding balance of the Accounts Receivable, Credit Card Companies account balance has not been recorded. This accrual entry will decrease the Accounts Receivable, Credit Card Companies account (**be sure to round to the nearest cent**).

In the past, Gold Run Snowmobile, Inc., has experienced small shortages (shrinkage) in merchandise inventory when the perpetual inventory total maintained on the computerized accounting system was compared to the actual physical inventory count taken at the end of the accounting period. When this shrinkage occurred, the Cost of Goods Sold account was debited and the Merchandise Inventory account was credited for the total value of the inventory shortage. The entry was followed by an update of the specific merchandise items where the quantities were not correct. At the end of the current quarter the physical count of merchandise on hand matches the perpetual inventory for each item in stock. As a result of the satisfactory inventory control system that is in place, no losses have occurred and no adjusting entry for inventory shrinkage is required this quarter.

When all of the adjusting entries have been correctly entered, PRINT THE ADJUSTED TRIAL BALANCE! The correct balance will be $\underline{\$848,794.55}$.

You are now ready to complete the final evaluation of the Gold Run Snowmobile, Inc., operations. **To gather the necessary information to complete the final evaluation questions, PRINT ALL of the documents listed in instructions 1-10.**

1. **Click on the Financial Statements tab. Click on the individual print icons and print the Income Statement, Retained Earnings Statement, and the Balance Sheet.**

THE CORRECT NET INCOME FOR GOLD RUN SNOWMOBILE, INCORPORATED, IS BETWEEN $\underline{\$58,400.00}$ AND $\underline{\$58,450.00}$.

2. **Click on the Subsidiary Ledgers tab and print the Schedule of Accounts Receivable.**

3. **Click on the Print All icon and print the Accounts Receivable Subsidiary Ledger.**

4. **Click on the Accounts Payable View Schedule icon and print the Schedule of Accounts Payable.**

5. **Click on the Print All icon and print the Accounts Payable Subsidiary Ledger.**

6. **Click on the General Ledger tab. Click on the Red Snowmobile icon and print a copy the Inventory Reorder Analysis.**

7. **Click on the Inventory Item icon and print the following inventory stock cards:**

        T1500   T2000   SW660   SSS30   LL466

        N6000   Z9000

The Closing process for the Gold Run Snowmobile accounting system is an automatic function. The program will close all of the temporary accounts and, at the same time, adjust the Merchandise Inventory account.

8. Click on the General Journal tab. Click on the <u>Closing</u> entries button and answer Yes. When the closing is completed, answer OK.

9. Click on the General Ledger tab and print the Post-Closing Trial Balance.

10. Click on the Ledger Account icon and print the following accounts:

    101 Cash
    105 Accounts Receivable
    107 Accounts Receivable, Credit Card Companies
    115 Merchandise Inventory
    201 Accounts Payable
    305 Retained Earnings
    401 Snowmobile, Accessories, & Parts Sales
    411 Service Fees Earned
    501 Cost of Goods Sold
    607 Credit Card Expense
    711 Interest Earned
    901 Income Summary

Exit the Gold Run Snowmobile, Incorporated, accounting program. Using all of your printed documents, carefully answer the Final Evaluation questions. The questions and several of the end-of-the-quarter documents may be collected by your instructor.

Error Correction After Closing the Books

If, after closing the books, you discover an error or wish to print a corrected copy of any of the financial statements, you must go to the **General Journal** and click on the **Restore** button. Answer **Yes** and then **OK** to restore the journal and ledgers to pre-closing balances. Daily or adjusting entries can then be corrected using the **<u>Daily</u> Entries** or **<u>Adjusting</u> Entries** option and then **new copies of all corrected documents <u>MUST</u> be printed.** Again, close the books, print a corrected **Post-Closing Trial Balance,** and any corrected general ledger accounts. Then exit the program.

FINAL EVALUATION

GOLD RUN SNOWMOBILE, INC.

December 31, 2001

FINAL EVALUATION

GOLD RUN SNOWMOBILE, INC.

NAME_____

SECTION_____ DATE_____

1. Does the balance of the Schedule of Accounts Receivable match the Accounts Receivable account balance? YES_____ NO_____

2. Which customer has the smallest outstanding balance on December 31? (Identify by customer number.) _____

3. A credit memo was issued to Mary Bermuda on December 16. What was the number of the sales invoice for this transaction? _____

4. What amount of the balance owed by the Running Ramblers is past due? (Gold Run Snowmobile, Inc. extends net 30 credit terms to all customers.) $_____

5. Which customer charged merchandise on account on December 21? (Identify by customer number.) _____

6-7. What is the invoice number and the vendor number of the December 21 entry to Accounts Payable? Invoice_____

Vendor Number_____

8. By what date should the Inglass, Inc., balance be paid? Date_____

9. The Morelli Sports Equipment debit memo was for a return of merchandise from what original purchase invoice number? Invoice_____

10. What was the balance owed to Morelli Sports Equipment before the posting of the debit memo? $_____

11. If the Trail-Tracker, Inc., account is not paid in full within the discount period for each of the outstanding invoices, what will be the total amount of the discounts lost? $_____

12. Examine the Fastwinn, Incorporated account. In order to take the discount offered, which outstanding invoice must be paid in full no later than January 6? Invoice Number_____

13. How much cash was paid out on December 26? $_____

14-15. A Swift, Incorporated purchase invoice was paid in full on December 30. What was the number of the invoice paid and the number of the check that was issued for payment? Invoice Number_____

Check Number_____

16-17. Check number 30116 was issued on what date and for what amount? Date_____

$_____

18. What was the reason for the December 17 credit entry of $6,000 to the Cash Account?

_____

FINAL EVALUATION
GOLD RUN SNOWMOBILE, INC.

19. For the month of December, how many Service Fees Earned transactions were charged by customers? _____

20. How many inventory items are now out of stock? _____

21. How many inventory items with **only three** units in stock are at or below the reorder point? _____

22. How many CC100 units are in stock? _____

23. How many Trail-Tracker 1500 units were issued (sold) during December? _____

24-25. On what date were the fifteen pairs of competition gloves (LL466) purchased and from which vendor were they acquired?

    Date _____

    Vendor Number _____

26. The two T2000 units sold on December 13 were reported sold on what sales invoice? (Identify by number.) _____

27. What is the FIFO inventory value of the 35 Neon Caps (N6000) in stock? $_____

28. What is the FIFO inventory value of stock number SSS30? $_____

29. Under a perpetual inventory system, if the LIFO method of inventory valuation was used, what would be the inventory value of stock number SSS30? $_____

30. Under a periodic inventory system, if the LIFO method of inventory valuation was used, what would be the inventory value of stock number SSS30? $_____

31. A total of 21 Trail-Tracker snowmobiles are currently in stock. What is the total amount of cash tied up in this inventory at this time? $_____

32. If the transportation-in costs had been reduced to zero through more successful negotiation of merchandise contracts, what would be the corrected Gross Profit From Sales? $_____

Round all percentage answers to two decimal positions (4.57689% = 4.58%).

33. Total cost of goods sold is what percent of Net Sales? _____%

34. Last quarter the Total Selling Expenses were 10.59% of total net revenues. Has this quarter, ending December 31, 2001, been an improvement over last quarter?   YES_____ NO_____

35. Salaries and Wages Expense is what percent of the total net revenues (net sales and fees earned)? _____%

FINAL EVALUATION
GOLD RUN SNOWMOBILE, INC.

36. Compared to December 3 (beginning merchandise inventory balance), the December 31 ending merchandise inventory has increased by what percent? _____%

37. What is the book value of Store Equipment and Fixtures? $_____

38. Does Gold Run Snowmobile have enough cash on hand to meet current liabilities? YES_____ NO_____

39. What is the Net Accounts Receivable balance? $_____

40. If an additional $500 was written off as an uncollectible bad debt, what would be the new Net Accounts Receivable balance? $_____

41. On the December 31, 2001 Balance Sheet, what is the "net worth" (total stockholders' equity) of the business? $_____

42. After closing, what is the balance of Dividends Declared? $_____

43. What has been the **Net** increase in Retained Earnings this quarter? $_____

44. What must be the last account listed on the Gold Run Snowmobile Post-Closing Trial Balance? _____

45. After closing, what is the balance of the Income Summary account? $_____

46. If the total for Service Fees Earned and Storage Fees Earned could be increased by 25% with only a $450 increase in Salaries and Wages Expense and a $350 increase in Advertising Expense, what would be the new total for Income From Operations? $_____

47. If $800 of Delivery Expense charges were found to be recorded in the Transportation In account, the Cost of Goods Sold and Gross Profit would change by $800. If this error was corrected, what would be the corrected balance of the Net Income? $_____

48. If it was discovered that the December 26 purchase invoice from Trail-Tracker had not been entered on the books, but the merchandise had been counted in the ending inventory, would Gross Profit be overstated, understated, or unchanged? _____

49. If an audit determined that due to "shrinkage" the ending inventory was overstated by $1,500, would the reported Net Income of the business be overstated, understated, or unchanged? _____

50. If "shrinkage" of $1,000 was reported after the inventory was officially counted on December 31, 2001, the Merchandise Inventory account would be credited for the $1,000. The missing inventory item/s would be accounted for in the entry and the perpetual inventory system would be brought up-to-date. In the journal entry, what account would be debited for the shrinkage? _____

APPENDIX

Gold Run Snowmobile, Inc.
Trial Balance
December 3, 2001

	Debit	Credit
Cash	$ 24,834.30	
Petty Cash	50.00	
Short-Term Investments	14,150.00	
Accounts Receivable	36,697.22	
Allow. Doubt. Accounts		$ 734.50
Accts. Rec., Credit Card Co.	7,641.75	
Notes Receivable	9,600.00	
Merchandise Inventory	109,164.77	
Prepaid Insurance	4,220.00	
Prepaid Property Tax	660.00	
Store and Shop Supplies	2,145.00	
Store Equipment and Fixtures	51,700.00	
Accum. Deprec., Store Eq. & Fix.		15,200.00
Shop Equipment	20,250.00	
Accum. Deprec., Shop Equip.		6,750.00
Trucks	28,200.00	
Accum. Deprec., Trucks		6,750.00
Land	109,500.00	
Leasehold	16,000.00	
Accounts Payable		42,878.00
Notes Payable		13,000.00
Sales Tax Payable		2,306.00
Dividends Payable		11,500.00
Unearned Storage Fees		10,100.00
Long-Term Lease Liability		6,500.00
Discount on Lease Financing	1,008.41	
Common Stock		250,000.00
Retained Earnings		58,195.45
Dividends Declared	11,500.00	
Snowmobile and Acces., Sales		137,650.00
Sales Returns & Allowances	1,517.00	
Service Fees Earned		9,765.00
Cost of Goods Sold	80,100.00	
Transportation-In	615.00	
Salaries and Wages Expense	17,015.00	
Truck & Equip. Operating Exp.	812.95	
Advertising Expense	1,715.00	
Delivery Expense	535.00	
Credit Card Expense	805.00	
Tools Expense	50.00	
Rent Expense	12,000.00	
Electric and Gas Expense	801.05	
Telephone Expense	423.00	
Bank Service Charges	65.00	
License Expense	316.00	
Professional Services Expense	413.00	
Cash Short & Over	16.00	
Discounts Lost	34.00	
Miscellaneous Expense	91.50	
Interest Earned		312.00
Dividends Earned		119.00
Miscellaneous Revenue		40.00
Income Taxes Expense	6,835.00	
Interest Expense	319.00	
Total	$ 571,799.95	$ 571,799.95

Gold Run Snowmobile, Inc.
Schedule of Accounts Receivable
Last Activity Date: December 3, 2001

Number	Name	Balance
10400	Mary Bermuda	$ .00
10450	Colfax Sno Katts	.00
10750	Alice Cordero	.00
10930	Downieville Dusters	2,550.00
11000	Chris Enburger	435.00
11250	Cathi Grobowski	842.00
11340	Beverly Kline	.00
11470	Ray Norburg	5,712.22
11510	Karen Osetto	.00
11675	Cheryl Papini	398.00
11780	Running Ramblers	6,215.00
11800	Snowbirds	.00
11925	Thunder Mountain, Inc.	.00
11950	Ruth Yates	20,545.00
Total		$ 36,697.22

Gold Run Snowmobile, Inc.
Schedule of Accounts Payable
Last Activity Date: December 3, 2001

Number	Name	Balance
20300	Buster Supply	.00
21680	Butler & Kadnaso	14,795.00
22500	Fastwinn, Incorporated	.00
23400	Inglass, Incorporated	.00
24850	Morelli Sports Equipment	5,200.00
26500	Norton America	15,741.00
27000	Swift, Incorporated	.00
28400	Trail-Tracker, Inc.	.00
29650	Wind Dancer	7,142.00
Total		$ 42,878.00

Gold Run Snowmobile, Inc.

Inventory Analysis
Last Activity Date: December 2

Stock Number	Inventory Item	Reorder Point	Units On Hand	Unit Cost	At/Below Reorder
T1500	TRAIL-TRACKER 1500	2	4	$4,116.00	
T2000	TRAIL-TRACKER 2000	3	4	5,148.00	
T3000	TRAIL-TRACKER 3000	3	2	5,390.00	Yes
T3300	TRAIL-TRACKER ENDURO	1	3	6,860.00	
SW660	SWIFT ENDURO	1	2	5,940.00	
SW999	SWIFT ARROW	1	0	9,900.00	Yes
SS100	NORTON TRAILER SOLO	2	12	490.00	
SD200	NORTON TRAILER DUO	2	8	693.00	
SSS30	QUAD HAULER	2	0	1,188.00	Yes
A1000	SNOWBOUND BATTERY	4	14	30.50	
A1150	SUPER CHARGER BATTER	4	12	49.50	
B1200	TIE DOWNS KIT	4	5	19.50	
B1340	ENDURO ENGINE COWL	1	2	56.00	
B2250	MAGNETO ASSEMBLY	2	0	94.50	Yes
B3000	CUSTOM DECAL KIT	5	30	32.00	
B4400	MUFFLER PAK	3	8	65.30	
B5600	OIL PUMP ASSEMBLE	1	3	64.50	
B7777	LUGGAGE CARRIER	2	4	38.00	
CC100	STANDARD SHOCK	9	20	17.50	
CC555	SUPER DUTY SHOCK	9	3	27.25	Yes
EE222	FUEL TANK 6 GALLON	2	5	6.40	
J1001	M WIND TEK SUIT MD	3	1	150.00	Yes
J2002	M WIND TEK SUIT LG	3	4	160.00	
J3003	M WIND TEK SUIT XLG	3	8	175.00	
J7777	W WIND TEK SUIT SM	3	5	120.00	
J8888	W WIND TEK SUIT MD	3	14	130.00	
J9999	W WIND TEK SUIT LG	3	12	140.00	
LL244	SNOW MITTENS MEDIUM	6	8	20.25	
LL355	SNOW MITTENS LARGE	6	12	22.40	
LL466	COMPETITION GLOVES	4	3	79.00	Yes
M0300	W TRAIL BOOTS	6	6	55.00	Yes
M0440	M TRAIL BOOTS	6	4	65.00	Yes
M0555	RACING SHIRT	6	13	16.50	
M1500	THERMAL SHIRT MD	6	0	14.25	Yes
M1650	THERMAL SHIRT LG	4	7	16.25	
M2222	TUFF TURTLES	0	18	8.75	
M3344	TUFF TURTLES H WT.	0	16	11.25	
N6000	NEON CAP	0	36	6.00	
N7500	KNIT CAPS	9	32	12.75	

Inventory Analysis
Last Activity Date: December 2

Stock Number	Inventory Item	Reorder Point	Units On Hand	Unit Cost	At/Below Reorder
RR222	THERMAL FACEMASK	4	9	13.30	
RR300	RACING FACEMASK	2	12	24.40	
RR404	CRUZE HELMET	3	6	65.50	
RR555	DELUXE RACING HELMET	6	25	95.00	
RR900	HELMET BAG	2	3	21.25	
RR925	CRUZE FACESHIELD	4	1	9.90	Yes
RR933	FOGGER FACESHIELD	4	6	12.40	
RR999	HOT GRIPS	4	8	28.50	
U0001	ACE GOGGLES	4	4	22.60	Yes
U0012	SPORT GLASSES	4	3	7.40	Yes
U1000	MICRO WINDSHIELD	1	1	44.10	Yes
U2200	FANNY PAKS	5	25	17.25	
V0333	SNOWMOBILE COVER	2	1	58.80	Yes
V4400	SADDLE BAGS	2	2	36.00	Yes
W1111	SPEEDOMETER	2	12	29.40	
W7777	TACHOMETER	2	2	31.36	Yes
XX111	GEARLUBE 1-GALLON	2	5	6.25	
XX222	CRUZE OIL CASE	4	12	9.00	
XX333	HOTSHOT OIL CASE	4	4	32.00	Yes
Z9000	TEAM TR-TRACKER BAG	1	0	22.00	Yes
ZZ100	TRAIL-TRACKER JACKET	2	2	63.50	Yes

Items At or Below Reorder Point: 20

Total Value of Inventory: $109,164.77